DREAMS
AND
DICTATORS

DREAMS AND DICTATORS

On the Book of Daniel

HERMAN VELDKAMP

PAIDEIA PRESS

www.paideiapress.ca

Dreams and Dictators
First published in Dutch
as *In de schemering van Christus' wederkomst*
by T. Wever of Franeker.
Translated by Theodore Plantinga.

This English edition is a publication of Paideia Press (3248 Twenty First St., Jordan Station, Ontario, Canada L0R 1S0), a publishing imprint of the Cántaro Institute. Copyright ©2024 by Paideia Press. All rights reserved.

Except for brief quotations in critical publications or reviews, no part of this book may be reproduced in any manner without prior written permission from Paideia Press at the address above.

Copy-editing: Paul Aurich
Book Design by: Steven R. Martins

ISBN 978-0-88815-355-5

Printed in the United States of America

Table of Contents

1. Change of Name ... 7
2. Putting Faith into Practice ... 17
3. God's Holy Laughter ... 25
4. Babylon's Bankruptcy ... 33
5. The Talent of Prayer ... 41
6. The Talent of Revelation ... 49
7. Man's Empire and God's Kingdom ... 57
8. God's Festival of Sacrifice ... 67
9. Nebuchadnezzar's Hallelujah ... 77
10. Thou Art the Man! ... 87
11. The Human Beast ... 97
12. Multiplied Peace ... 105
13. What Belshazzar Forgot ... 113
14. What God Did Not Forget ... 123
15. Applause or Amen? ... 133
16. The Plot Against Prayer ... 143
17. Prayer's Response ... 153
18. Perseverance in Prayer ... 163
19. Prayer's Victory ... 173

20.	Four Monsters in a Dream	181
21.	Unholy and Holy Aggression	191
22.	The Throne in Heaven	201
23.	The Fourth Empire	209
24.	The Things to Come—the World	217
25.	The Things to Come—the Church	227
26.	The Final Outcome	235
27.	Come, Lord Jesus!	245
28.	A Humble Attitude	253
29.	In God's Inner Chamber	263
30.	In the Devil's Headquarters	273
31.	Before the Antichrist	281
32.	The Disastrous Abomination	291
33.	Great Was His Fall!	299
34.	Deliverance	307
35.	How Long?	315

1

Change of Name

*The chief eunuch gave them other names,
calling Daniel Belteshazzar, Hananiah
Shadrach, Mishael Meshach, and Azariah
Abednego (1:7 JB).*

THE KING'S CHIEF EUNUCH, as we read in Daniel 1:3, was Ashpenaz. We are told that he had a steward or overseer working under him (vs. 11).

I don't propose to take up the question just what kind of high office this chief eunuch held in the Babylonian empire. Suffice to say that he was in charge of youth work in this well-organized state—or that supervising the youth work was a very important part of his responsibilities. He discharged this responsibility conscientiously, for the love of organization was in his blood. He saw to it that his carefully thought-out system was applied even in the smallest particulars: no detail was too insignificant to be worthy of his scrutiny.

His job was to inject the heathen Babylonian spirit into the minds and hearts of the Israelite youths who had been imported from Jerusalem. These children of the covenant were supposed to become totally Babylonian in their outlook and conduct. Included in the set of regulations adopted to achieve this goal was this measure that concerns us in this chapter, that is, the change of name reported in our text.

That name change was not a mere whim on the part of this minister of education. He did not change the names of these youths primarily because such names as Belteshazzar, Shadrach, Meshach and Abednego would sound better to the Babylonians at the court. No, his motives went much deeper than that!

But first let's try to find out what is actually at stake in the book of Daniel. What is this book all about?

The background to the book of Daniel is laid out very clearly in the first three verses:

In the third year of the reign of Jehoiakim king of Judah, Nebuchadnezzar king of Babylon came to Jerusalem and besieged it. And the Lord gave Jehoiakim king of Judah into his hand, with some of the vessels of the house of God; and he brought them to the land of Shinar, to the house of his god, and placed the vessels in the treasury of his god. Then the king commanded Ashpenaz, his chief eunuch, to bring some of the people of Israel, both of the royal family and of the nobility.

Now, if we look at this purely as a historical statement, all we see is that some Babylonian troops besiege Jerusalem at a certain time, that Jerusalem fell to them, and that Nebuchadnezzar, the king of Babylon, took some of the treasures of Israel's temple away and placed them instead in a temple in Shinar, where idols were worshipped. That's how conquerors acted in those days. They wanted to show that the people as well as the gods of the victorious nation were too strong to be resisted. Furthermore, we read that Nebuchadnezzar carried away not only the holy vessels of the House of God but also some holy people. These captives were taken to Babylon too.

When we recall that the book of Daniel is a *prophetic* book even in its historical sections, our eyes are immediately opened to the implication of Nebuchadnezzar's policy. In the very first verse of the book of Daniel, we read about Jerusalem and Babylon. Thus, we are aware from the outset that Daniel's struggle is another battle in the great war between Jerusalem and Babylon (the Greek version of the name) or Babel (the Hebrew version). Jerusalem is the city of God; it is the capital of the "Kingdom of heaven." Babylon, however, is the headquarters of the kingdom of darkness. In the revelation to John, which is a classic book of prophecy, these two also stand opposed. On the one hand we have Babylon, and on the other hand the Jerusalem that descends from heaven.

The author of the book of Daniel deliberately uses the old name *Shinar* to remind us of the origin of this world power that arises in opposition to God. It was on the plains of Shinar that mankind declared, "Come, let us build ourselves a city, and a tower with its top in the heavens" (Gen. 11:4). Shinar was where man sought to make a name for himself by building the great tower of Babel.

Jerusalem versus Babel is the great opposition that has dominated world history throughout the ages. It is a colossal struggle between the Kingdom of God and the kingdom of satan, the church and the world, the Christ and the Antichrist. Whereas John tells us in Revelation of the final battle and ultimate triumph of Christ, Daniel describes one of the many phases in the struggle.

What strikes us about this first chapter of Daniel is that the *youth* are quickly drawn into the struggle. Daniel and his friends were boys who could not have been much older than fourteen. These boys bore the brunt of the attack—an attack made not by force but by cunning. The plan was to win them for Babylon in a gentle, step by step way through a systematic procedure designed to transform them completely, a procedure too subtle to be easily recognizable.

These boys would have to be on their guard, then. And young men and women in our time must watch out as well. Nor should their parents be asleep, for although the crafty plan of Ashpenaz is old, it is by no means obsolete. On the contrary, it lives in many modernized forms in our time.

That's one of the reasons why the prophecy of Daniel is so relevant to our day. In our time as in Daniel's days, Nebuchadnezzar is even more interested in stealing people than treasures from the temple. And he takes a special interest in young people. Whoever succeeds in winning over the youth....

Now that we have a bird's eye view of the situation, we turn again to the strategy adopted by Ashpenaz. The change of name was an integral part of the procedure.

Nebuchadnezzar begins by ordering the deportation from Jerusalem of youths "both of the royal family and of the nobility." Naturally he is interested especially in the elite, the privileged few, the future leaders of the people, for what can a nation accomplish when its leading citizens are taken away? But the Babylonian ruler does not stop here: deporting the future leaders is not enough. He plans to bend them to his will and use them for his own purposes—which is a definite possibility with boys of that age. The character and convictions of such boys are not yet fixed and hardened. Therefore, someone like Nebuchadnezzar can make of them virtually anything he cares to.

Now, Nebuchadnezzar did not treat these captives of royal blood as prisoners! He did not lock them up in a concentration camp. Of course not! They would have gritted their teeth, clenched their fists, and cursed their conqueror in their hearts. No, Nebuchadnezzar turned his diplomats loose on them instead. These diplomats had much more refined ways of handling people. The Jewish youth were brought to Nebuchadnezzar's court, where they were accepted as members of the upper crust and given a model education. We read that they received thorough instruction in "the letter and language of the Chaldeans" (1:4).

What would have happened if the king had succeeded in turning these sons of Judah's royal house into Babylonians in body and in spirit? What if they had become Chaldeans and had been alienated from the religion, ethos and language of their own people? They would have exercised a pagan influence on the other Israelites, and it would not have been long before the Jewish nation, the people of the Lord, was completely swallowed up by the powerful Babylonian empire. The Jews would be digested and assimilated—that was the goal!

These boys first had to read much and learn much. They had to become familiar with the heathen beliefs and ideology of the Babylonians. That was the spiritual nourishment they were offered.

But even their daily menu of food and drink was prescribed: "The king assigned them a daily portion of the rich food which the king ate, and of the wine which he drank" (1:5).

The object was not that these boys should enjoy every

possible comfort and live a life of luxury in the palace. No, the rules about food were simply part of the system! Everything in the lives of these boys was to be transformed, including their diet. They would have to make a radical break with the past. Those old-fashioned Jewish regulations about food would be cast aside—together with all the other customs and habits of their fathers. The last threads tying them to their own people would have to be cut—hence the prescribed menu. In the excellent public education these boys received, it was laid out in minute detail just what they were to study, what they were to believe, what they were to eat, and even *how* they were to eat. It was all part of the system.

The old Russian city of Saint Petersburg has been renamed Leningrad. Another Russian city became Stalingrad and has since been renamed again. Are these changes insignificant? Not in the least! Everything that reminded people of the old regime in Russia had to disappear. Therefore, the names of streets, squares and cities were changed.

Daniel and his friends, likewise, also needed new names. There was something of the name of God to be heard in the names of these four boys. *Daniel* means *God is judge!* Surely such a name could not be tolerated! These youths would have to bear the names that sang the praises of the Babylonian idols. There was to be no mention of God's name in Babylon.

We can thank God that this Babylonian system of public education has not yet been established in our country, although there are other countries where it is imposed as the highest form of human wisdom. But who is to say how long we will remain free from such practices? Many attempts are already being made to secularize the youth, to make them breathe this spirit of the world. Sometimes this even goes on unnoticed within our homes and families.

What are we doing to defend ourselves? Let's begin by recalling the fact that our sons and daughters are also members of a "royal family": they are children of God, members of God's household. Consequently, we, too, have been subjected to a change of name. We are no longer called "children of wrath": we are called "Christians," for we confess the name of *Christ!*

But how in the world are our children to become confessors of God's name and bearers of his banner if even their parents teach them the wisdom and letters and language of the Chaldeans? We push our children to get a top-notch education so that they will be able to find a good job and carve out a place for themselves in society! We make them study all sorts of things and read all kinds of books. Yet we don't bother to find out whether they read the Book of books, whether they understand the language of faith, or whether they know that the fear of the Lord is the beginning of wisdom. We have little time for youth work or for the church's instruction in the faith. Where are you to look for the modern-day Nebuchadnezzar who entices your children away from serving God? Have you looked for him in your favorite chair in front of the TV set?

Why are you called a Christian? You're a Christian not just to receive instruction and read the scriptures but first and foremost to love God in a priestly way. That's the chief need of our time, of young people and older people alike. It's not enough to be at home in the Bible: we must devote ourselves *completely* to the Lord.

For Christians the Bible is not just a study book or a book of sermons or a book to read in church: it's a handbook that we consult every morning before we go to work. It's the word of God, and therefore we listen to it eagerly and attentively! "Speak, Lord, for Your servant is listening. Teach me to act in accordance with Your will and to walk in the light of Your truth." Then Babylon will not prove too strong for Jerusalem. Then the world's attack will fail even if it is directed against 14-year-olds like Daniel. "Out of the mouth of babes and sucklings hast thou ordained *strength*"! (Ps. 8:2 KJV).

2

Putting Faith Into Practice

But Daniel resolved that he would not defile himself with the king's rich food, or with the wine which he drank; therefore, he asked the chief of the eunuchs to allow him not to defile himself (1:8).

DANIEL IS ONE OF THE HEROES of the faith. When the author of the letter to the Hebrews parades the leaders in the Kingdom of God before our eyes, we see Daniel in their ranks. True, his name is not mentioned, but we add him automatically in our thoughts when we are reminded of those who through faith "stopped the mouths of lions." Isn't that what Daniel did? Whenever Daniel is mentioned, we think of the night he spent in the lions' den. What a man he was! What an example he set in his faith, spending a night in the company of lions just as calmly as if he were in his own bedroom!

We think less often of the heroism that Daniel displayed in the dining room of Nebuchadnezzar's palace. Nevertheless, what he did there required just as much courage. We should remember that the devil is an ever-greater danger in the world's dining rooms than in the dens of lions. When we hear the sounds of the king's meal being served, when we hear the glasses clink, we should be even more on our guard than when famished lions open their mouths. Be careful what you do when you are near the kitchen, Daniel. The stomach can be satan's instrument.

Now, Daniel was indeed on his guard. He "resolved in his heart that he would not defile himself with the king's rich food or with wine which he drank." It was as though he already saw the roaring lion padding across the inland floors of the royal palace—even before his encounter with those other lions. If Daniel had not been faithful to God while seated at the King's table, he would never have survived the lions' den. How could he be faithful in such a great matter if he had not been faithful in little things first?

Thus, it is through the daily menu that we first catch a glimpse of Daniel's courage, courage rooted in faith. He shows us how to put godliness into *practice*. This example is more applicable to most of us. Venturing into lions' dens, after all, is reserved for a very small minority. Very few of us will ever have the frightful blessing of glorifying God in the presence of hungry lions.

Of course, we have no idea what may yet happen to us in the future, but for now we should concern ourselves with today. And what is asked of us now is that we put our faith into practice when it comes to what takes place in the dining room—in the living room, in the bedroom. In other words, we must concern ourselves for the present with our daily life at school, in the office, on the street, in the bank—in short, wherever our day-to-day business happens to take us. It makes little sense to torment ourselves with the question of whether we could live up to the example that Daniel set in the lions' den (chapter 5) if we do not first take our place beside him in the dining room (chapter one) and resolutely refuse to consume anything that might defile us.

For many of us it is far from obvious what is at issue in the dining room. Because of this, there is something terribly sad about the first chapter of Daniel. Certainly, it is nice that Daniel and his friends abstained from the tasty dishes and sparkling wines. The story is actually quite interesting, for as it turns out, the boys who lived on bread and water eventually appeared healthier than the others who ate rich food from the king's table. But there were only four who abstained—Daniel and his three friends. It is clear that the initiative for this venture came from one of them, Daniel, and that it was his courageous faith that carried the others along. But where were all the other sons of the royal family and of the nobility who had been brought from Judah? We are left with the impression that many fell quickly into line with Nebuchadnezzar's intentions. They probably thought Daniel far too rigid: he was overdoing it! There has to be room for some give and take. Who would be so foolish as to spoil everything for himself? Why would anyone want to undermine his own security and future—especially when a little flexibility would accomplish so much more? Surely no one could interpret their eating the king's food and drinking his wine to mean that they had given up the faith of their fathers!

That's why I pointed out earlier that it is far from obvious to everyone that we are to bring our faith to bear on the question of what we should eat and drink!

Now we must take a closer look at what is at stake in the matter of eating the king's food and drinking his wine. Of course, we must be careful not to look at this matter in a superficial way. Anyone who judges the matter lightly will quickly conclude that Daniel's course of action was childish. After all, what could be wrong with eating those fine foods? Why had God created wine if he didn't intend us to drink it? Why was it so important for Daniel and his friends to live on bread and water? Surely the Bible doesn't teach that we must all be vegetarians and teetotalers! Come on, Daniel, don't be so fussy! You may take offence at all sorts of little things, but we find your whole attitude offensive. Your kind of outlook has already led to enough trouble. The Pharisees, too, were much too scrupulous to defile themselves by entering Pilate's courtroom, but their scruples did not stop them from plotting murder! We want nothing to do with such people! Those Pharisees were like whitewashed tombs: their outward appearance was beautiful, but they were full of dead man's bones!

Now, if Daniel had been one of those Pharisees, we would have good reason to be suspicious of his resolve not to "defile" himself. But he wasn't! I pointed out earlier that Nebuchadnezzar's intention in forcing his menu on the Jewish youths was to make them forget all about the customs and dietary regulations of their forefathers. It was all part of his system. Their way of life would have to be transformed down to the smallest details. The food on the table was an important aspect of the new way of life. Thus, for Nebuchadnezzar, the new menu was no minor detail. And on this point Daniel agreed with him.

But that's still not all there was to it. The Babylonians were not acquainted with our modern saying that religion is a private matter. On the contrary, they believed that all of life is permeated by religion. The foods eaten at the meals were first offered to the gods. Every meal took on the character of a "holy" meal, a kind of idolatrous sacrament. Apparently, the rule was: whether you are eating or drinking or doing something else, do it all to the glory of Babylon's gods.

This puts us to shame! After all, how many of us would open a meal by declaring that God is the host at our table?

How many of us really eat and drink, buy and sell, build and plant to the glory of God? How many of us devote our *entire* lives to a service? We all recognize the church as an area in which God is to be served, but it is surrounded by all that wide open territory in which we go about our own business and lead our own lives. Religion is religion and belongs in the church—but business is business!

Hence those meals eaten in Nebuchadnezzar's palace should make us feel ashamed. But now we also understand why the four friends resisted from the outset. The matter wasn't as simple as it looked at first glance. If they joined in Babylon's meals, they would begin to estrange themselves from their own faith. Therefore, Daniel felt that he had to put his faith into practice at the dinner table!

He went about it in a very sensible way. He didn't create a scene, and he didn't strike the pose of a martyr. Some people believe that firmness of principles always involves acting stubborn and pigheaded, but Daniel was not one of them. He began with a friendly inquiry. When the chief eunuch turned down his request on the grounds that granting such a favor might well cost him his life, Daniel did not respond with a joke or a haughty remark. He put himself in the position of this heathen official and let him know that he could appreciate his difficulty. He then went on to make the same request of someone lower in the chain of command—the steward. Daniel asked for a ten-day trial period, which surely could do little harm, as the four youths were scheduled to remain at the king's table for *three full years*. This was the sensible approach that Daniel used in faith to get his way with the "world."

This simple application of this story is not that we should follow Daniel's example by living on bread and water, but that we should put our faith into practice in the little things of everyday life. We should abide by our own God honoring way of life and draw on the power of Christ to struggle against the customs, forms, and manners of this world. This is not a matter of living like hermits or avoiding the world; it is rather, a matter of consecration.

Anyone who thinks of the evil of conforming to the world *exclusively* in terms of frequenting the world's dining rooms, dance halls, and fashion shows is making a serious mistake. This is not to deny that visiting such locales and reading worldly magazines and books actually amounts to conforming to the world in many cases, but the evil is more deeply rooted. The danger is this, that we derive the norms for our thought and conduct *not* from the scriptures but from the "world." These two sets of norms are completely opposed to each other. Forgiving our neighbors again and again, regarding our brothers and sisters as better than ourselves, praying for our enemies and business competitors, treating others as we would have them treat us—all these things are the dietary regulations of the church; they are the bread and water on which the church subsists.

My fear is that we have already banished the unappetizing diet from the table long ago. In this respect the first chapter of Daniel gives us reason to grieve, for it tells us of four young men who still clung to this simple diet, even though all others regard them as peculiar ascetics and mystics. Away with all the mysticism! We have more than enough scruples. We're much too worried about being defiled. We pile command upon command, rule upon rule, doctrine upon doctrine. Why don't you talk a little less about putting godliness into practice? Such talk sounds far too moralistic!

3

God's Holy Laughter

*Now Daniel was there till the
first year of King Cyrus (1:21 NEB).*

WE HEAR SOME HOLY LAUGHTER in the final verse of Daniel 1. "He who sits in the heavens laughs," declares the psalmist (Ps. 2:4), and once we are seated with Christ in heaven, as Paul explains it so calmly to the people of Ephesus, we, too, will be able to laugh with Him at the futile effort of the great powers that seek to harm Zion. But we will be laughing through our tears.

The author of the book of Daniel must have rejoiced in the Lord when he wrote: "Now Daniel was there till the first year of king Cyrus." Satan's plan, after all, was to see to it that Daniel did *not* remain—at least, not as the prophet of the Lord's speaking to Babylon's court of the name and glory of Israel's God. As we saw earlier, things had been so arranged that the name of Israel and its God would disappear as quickly and completely as possible. That's why Daniel and his three friends had to assume heathen names and had to eat Babylonian (material and spiritual) food. The intent was that they would live in the presence of the king as true Babylonians, having forgotten their earlier nation and religion.

But the wise men and rulers of Babylon forgot one thing, namely, that the Lord had claimed Daniel long before Nebuchadnezzar did. The Lord had chosen him to live at the court of the great king. In holy humour God's plan for Daniel undid all that Nebuchadnezzar had hoped to accomplish through his carefully thought-out program of education. According to Nebuchadnezzar's plan, Daniel was to cease his prophetic activity, but according to God's plan, he was to continue serving as His prophet and continue he did!

Daniel arrived in Babylon as a 14-year-old boy and remained there until he was an old man of 90. Nebuchadnezzar was long gone by then. Also gone was his mighty empire, the great Babylon he had built. But Daniel remained. Kings came and went—but Daniel remained. World empires rose and fell—but Daniel remained. He remained till the first year of king Cyrus, which was the year that an edict was issued allowing the exiles to return to their own land. Thus, Daniel even lived to see the day of liberation, the day when the people of the Lord were set free again! The harp was taken out of the willow tree as the captives liberated by the Lord headed for Jerusalem in a joyous procession. They returned to the city of the great King, the city they had not been able to forget.

> When Yahweh brought Zion's captives home,
> at first it seemed like a dream;
> then our mouths filled with laughter
> and our lips with song (Ps. 126:1-2 JB).

That's the laughter we were just talking about, the laughter akin to God's laughter. The attempts to destroy God's people through force, through the fiery furnace, and then through the savage lions in their den had all failed. Daniel lived through it all. All those storms broke over his head; he was tossed about on the billows and the waves. But Daniel remains. He remains until the hour of liberation finally arrived and his aged eyes opened wide in amazement as he watched the bands of pilgrims departing for Jerusalem. The beaten and the battered ship of the church had finally made it into a safe harbor.

He who sits in the heavens will laugh, and the mouths of all whom He has redeemed will be filled with laughter as well. The laughter and jubilation surrounding this amazing conclusion to a chapter full of threats and crafty plots reminds us of the joyous finale of an oratorio.

Daniel remained. It's a historical fact. But it's a fact with prophetic significance. The church of all ages is promised that whatever storms may break over our heads, Zion's foundations will not be washed away. The turbulence of the sea will never make the ship of the church capsize. The tricks and plots of the rulers of this earth will never destroy the church. Even if the churches are plundered and concentration camps are established, even if wars break out and there are earthquakes in various places, it will make no difference. Or rather—it will make this difference: that kind of shaking and testing will build up the church. The thunder and lightning and affliction depicted in the book of Revelation is God's way of leading up to the end, to that happy ending of the drama when Jerusalem descends from heaven. This Jerusalem is the city of which the psalmists spoke: "There is a river whose streams gladden the city of God, which the Most High has made his holy dwelling" (Ps. 46:4 NEB).

Indeed, just as Daniel persevered until the time of Cyrus, when the emancipation proclamation was issued, so the church will persevere, however much it may be attacked and persecuted. The church will live to see the day when the greatest of all kings proclaims in the edict of eternal deliverance. Mountains may move and hills may shake, that is, all earthly things that seem so firmly established may be overthrown, but God assures us that His covenant of peace will never waver, that's the promise our merciful God gives us.

This was the message of Daniel's prophecy while he remained at the Babylonian court. It applies to the church of the Lord too. Whether it applies to each one of us individually depends on whether we are *living* members of that church. The living members will surely remain, for all those who do the will of God will abide forever.

We have not yet exhausted the divine humor in the concluding verse of Daniel 1. Daniel remained at the court—and not as a forgotten figure. He was rather a man of great influence, for he had become the chief of the wise men.

Just see how God's plans go directly contrary to the plans of Nebuchadnezzar. What happened many years later? "Now when Jesus was born in Bethlehem of Judea in the days of Herod the king, behold, wise men from the east came to Jerusalem saying, 'Where is he who has been born king of the Jews? For we have seen his star in the East, and have come to worship him'" (Matt. 2:1). How in the world could these astrologers from the East have arrived at the idea that the star they saw was *His* star, the star signaling the birth of the "king of the Jews"? It all makes sense when we recall that earlier Eastern astrologers were acquainted with Daniel, who prophesied that a star would arise over Jacob and the scepter over Israel.

Thus, God defeated Nebuchadnezzar with his own weapons. The king had commanded that Daniel be brought up in the wisdom of the Chaldeans so that he would learn to bow before the idols of Babylon, but God so arranged things that because of Daniel's place among the astrologers, wise men from the East would later come and bow down to the Christ. The books of the Chaldeans were supposed to draw Daniel away from God, but it turned out instead that the Chaldeans were drawn into the great Book, for the wise men from the East prompted the chief priests and scribes in Jerusalem to search the Scriptures: in the prophecy of Micah, they read that the Christ would be born in Bethlehem of Judea. He who sits in the heavens shall laugh!

Not only did those 14-year-old boys succeed in beating back hells furious assault, they even went over to the offensive. They themselves did not live to see the beautiful story of the wise men who knelt in adoration before the Savior, but the seed they scattered germinated and took root.

We should view this chapter as an inspiring story of evangelism. It should encourage the laborers on the mission field to keep up the good work. Go right ahead and sow the Word of God! You don't see any fruit? Well, remember that the sower went forth to sow. Leave it to God to give the increase.

We could also say that this story is an example of how to bring the gospel to intellectuals. The believers in Babylon's *academy* certainly did not remain silent about Christ. Remember that academics have souls too, just as well as people from the slums and drunks on skid row.

I hope that we all recognize our calling now. In the first chapter of Daniel, we see something of the dynamic, the saving power of the gospel. We see believers defending themselves and then taking the offensive. We see them refusing to defile themselves by eating food from the king's table. In other words, we see them taking pains to keep themselves unspotted from the world. But we also see them using their power in a quiet but forceful way to make the people at the court bow before the majesty of God's Word.

Both of these strategies are necessary. And if each is given the proper emphasis, God, who is seated in the heavens, will laugh. He will take holy delight in His obedient and willing people when He meets them in their splendid holy garments on the day of His glorious triumph.

4

Babylon's Bankruptcy

What your majesty requires of us is too hard; there is no one but the gods, who dwell remote from mortal men, who can give you the answer (2:11 NEB).

THE FIRST CHAPTER OF Daniel shows us Babylon's glory and majesty, the fullness of its power, and its organizational genius. But the second chapter describes Babylon's bankruptcy!

What has changed? Nothing! The conquered Jews did not rise up in rebellion, nor did any country declare war against this world empire. Nebuchadnezzar was just as firmly in the saddle as before. Thus, nothing had changed outwardly—except that Nebuchadnezzar had a dream. "Is that all?" we ask. Dreams are misleading and deceptive, and even if this were not so, there is a great gap between dreams and reality. That may be, yet this one dream was enough to cause an uproar in Babylon and call the existing order into question. A bomb attack from the sky could hardly have brought about more confusion in this world city than the invisible world of dreams did. Everything and everyone was upset.

The king was deeply worried about the dream: "His mind was so troubled that he could not sleep" (2:1 NEB). Because of his anxiety, he made wildly unreasonable demands of his wise men. These magicians, of course, stared back at the king blankly in their consternation, for they had no answer to the riddle of the dream; they had no way of probing this great mystery. The wise men were terrified—with good reason. Arioch, Babylon's chief executioner, had been commanded to cut these alleged wise men down to size—off with their heads!

All this was the result of a *dream*! God had spoken through the dark mysteries of sleep; He had pointed a finger at Nebuchadnezzar from a distance. What will happen to Babylon and other world empires when the dream is finally translated into awesome reality, when the Lord appears from the darkness of night and reveals his mighty arm? Then people will call upon mountains to fall upon them and hills to cover them.

Let's take a look at the world's bankruptcy. Nebuchadnezzar had a dream. In Daniel 2:1, we read that it happened in the *second* year of his reign. As we saw earlier, Daniel embarked on a course of studies *three* years in length. Therefore, he would still have been in the midst of his studies. Yet, when the wise men were unable to tell Nebuchadnezzar what he had dreamed, Daniel and his friends were to be put to death too. Evidently, they were included among the wise men. Moreover, at the end of the drama Daniel became a sort of "prime minister." Did all this happen when he was only sixteen years old? It seems to me that we are forced to conclude that the text has been corrupted, and that the original text speaks instead of the *twelfth* year of Nebuchadnezzar's reign.

But just what year it was is not all that important. More significant is the fact—and this emerges very clearly from the story—that even the most powerful rulers on this earth are pitiful figures. What fear and anxiety Nebuchadnezzar manifested! Why do rulers who control the destinies of millions ride in heavily guarded trains and bullet proof limousines? Why do they surround their palaces with high walls and armed guards?

Nebuchadnezzar was just as disturbed as the frightened rulers of our time. It was his dream especially that upset him. Daniel informed him: "The thoughts that came to you, O king, as you lay on your bed, were thoughts of things to come" (2:29 NEB). Of course, Nebuchadnezzar thought about the future, but what would the future bring? Would he be able to maintain his position in the face of internal unrest and foreign enemies? That's what he was brooding over. His worries were the troubled thoughts of a man who, although he was king, had no purpose in life, a man who had not become rich in the Lord. Such a person can never be at peace—especially not when his thoughts turn to "the things to come." Thus, Nebuchadnezzar's dream rose from his anxieties about the future, just as we probe and digest elements of the day's experiences in our dreams.

But there is one difference between our dreams and Nebuchadnezzar's dream: his was a revelation from God. God showed this monarch how shaky his throne was and how transitory his empire would be. Through this dream, the king's uneasiness and the anxiety in his palace were multiplied.

What does the king do after receiving this frightening vision? Where does he look for deliverance when God is busy pulling the rug out from under him? He does just what the world always does in times of upheaval. Each time his remedy is tried, it is found useless. Yet the world keeps right on writing the same prescription: seek help not from *God* but from *man*. And that's exactly what Nebuchadnezzar did. He looked to *human wisdom* to save the sinking ship of state; he believed that it would somehow be able to glue the shattered pieces back together again. In his predicament, in the uncertainty and confusion of the moment, he put his faith in the majesty of the human intellect. He held it fast with both hands. Man's wisdom was to give him back his peace of mind; a new day would dawn when the solution was found. "Then the king commanded the magicians, the enchanters, the sorcerers, and the Chaldeans to be summoned, to tell the king his dreams" (2:2).[1*]

There they stood before the king—magicians, enchanters, sorcerers, and Chaldeans! These scholars represented the four faculties of Babylon's academy. The theological faculty was not consulted. What would theologians like Daniel know about affairs of state? Let the preachers and priests—this is the same language spoken by modern Nebuchadnezzars—concern themselves with the afterlife and stay out of politics!

But the wise men could give the king no answer. In their desperation they made a clever attempt to get themselves out of the predicament by asking the king for the text before they gave the interpretation. But they were unable to supply both the text and the interpretation.

---

1   According to some translations, the Chaldeans spoke in Aramaic: "The Chaldeans, speaking Aramaic, said..." (2:4 NEB). Now, there is no reason why these Chaldeans should speak to their king in a foreign language. The words *in Aramaic* need to be put in brackets. Someone who made a copy of the text long ago apparently added them to indicate that the next part of the book of Daniel was written in Aramaic rather than Hebrew. By mistake, this marginal note was eventually incorporated into the text, leaving the reader with the comical impression that the Chaldeans suddenly started speaking Aramaic.

Now, Nebuchadnezzar was no fool. He wanted a firm guarantee that his counselors were not simply making up the interpretation, for the dream concerned important matters of state. If they would first tell him exactly what he had dreamed, he could then be sure that their interpretation was reliable. Nebuchadnezzar was on solid ground in making this demand, for the magicians had always maintained that they had a close relationship with the gods. Because of this relationship, it should not be difficult for them to come up with both the dream and its interpretation. It is clear from what the wise men said to the king that Nebuchadnezzar steadfastly refused to give them any details of the dream.

The wise men were dumbfounded. Their confusion spread from the palace throughout the entire academy. Babylon's scholars, politicians, statesmen, and professors were all perplexed. All of Babylon's wisdom was exposed as bankrupt, for God was busy breaking down the great empire that had been built up so carefully and painstakingly through continual wars and meticulous organization. Thus, the king had another problem to worry about—the failure of human wisdom!

From a psychological standpoint we can understand quite well why Nebuchadnezzar gave the command to put the wise men to death. They were not to be trusted. They might well be traitors and deceivers. Surely, they were a danger to the state. Away with them! All the king's former counselors would be swept away and disposed of.

This turn of events should not surprise us, for we have seen the same thing in our time. The world again stands on the edge of bankruptcy. We see unrest, uncertainty, and anxiety everywhere. In every area the old certainties are collapsing—in economics, politics, and religion. The once self-sufficient world has grown senile, tired, unsure. Like Nebuchadnezzar, it has awakened suddenly from a bad dream and can't get back to sleep. Our world, too, is tormented by thoughts of "the things to come."

Some people take malicious pleasure in this situation. "I told you so," they say. Others simply shake their heads and declare that the world is bankrupt, fully impoverished. Unfortunately, very few Christians understand that this gives the church a golden opportunity. The hour has come for another Daniel to step onto the stage! As long as Nebuchadnezzar is not afraid and the magicians are held in high esteem, Daniel will not be able to get a hearing. But now the great day has arrived for Daniel. He, too, is troubled and disturbed, but his uneasiness is a holy unrest. "Has the time finally come for me to proclaim the name of the Lord to kings and wise men?" he wonders.

Do we look for opportunities to make the name of Jesus Christ known? What do we do when the wall of modern man's supposed self-sufficiency, the wall that separates him from Christ, collapses? It may well be that the time has come for Jesus to make His approach to this world. What is the gospel but the point at which human misery and divine mercy meet?

Come, church of the Lord, step forward now with Daniel. Share with the whole world your knowledge, your insight into the divine mysteries. In the midst of the unrest and confusion of great and small, of kings and wise men, declare to the world what Daniel proclaimed in such a simple and naive way: "There is a God in heaven!"

5

The Talent of Prayer

Then Daniel went to his house and made the matter known to Hananiah, Mishael, and Azariah, his companions, and told them to seek the mercy of the Lord of heaven (2:17-18).

DANIEL ALREADY KNEW FROM experience what tremendous power there is in prayer. When storm clouds gather over our heads and danger surrounds us, we declare that it's time to pray, for we know that prayer should be our first resort rather than our last. Daniel was aware of this too. Yet he did not call an official prayer service in the church. The gathering was at Daniel's house, and the only people present were the four friends.

At this gathering the four did not *talk* at great length about the events of the day and the difficult circumstances in which they found themselves. Instead, they fell to their knees together. "Daniel then went home and told his friends Hananiah, Mishael, and Azariah what had happened, urging them to beg the God of heaven to show his mercy in this mysterious affair" (2:17-18 JB). Daniel's first thought was prayer!

The circumstances were certainly grave enough to call for prayer. You remember the situation. Nebuchadnezzar was uneasy because he was not sure whether his kingdom, which he had taken such pains to build up and strengthen, would be able to withstand internal unrest and foreign enemies. He became even more anxious when God came to him in the dream of the shattered statue and cast the future into still greater doubt. In his perplexity, Nebuchadnezzar looked to human intellect for help, but the wise men and political experts of Babylon were powerless to clarify the situation. He then made the confusion and anxiety in the land even greater by decreeing that all the wise men were to be put to death. The king hoped to disguise the gravity of the situation by rattling sabers. But official murder, of course, was no solution either.

Even the lives of Daniel and his three friends were endangered. For reasons not explained in the text, these four wise men had not been consulted. In a chilling way, they soon found out about the brutal, radical measures on which Nebuchadnezzar had decided: agents of Babylon's secret police appeared at the door to arrest them so that the death sentence could be carried out.

The appearance of police at the door did not cause Daniel to panic, although his life was indeed hanging by a slender thread. He was not as easily troubled in spirit as the king, for he knew something that Nebuchadnezzar did not know, namely, that God is our refuge and our strength, a timely help when we are in trouble. What happened to Daniel confirms the truth once more.

Daniel remained completely calm. We read: "When Arioch, the captain of the king's bodyguard, was setting out to execute the wise men of Babylon, Daniel approached him cautiously and with discretion" (2:14 NEB). This means simply that he inquired about the reason for all the executions. When he heard the explanation, he asked the king for a short stay of execution and his request was granted.

Daniel made good use of the time the king allowed him. He did not hold a conference with the king or with the other wise men of Babylon, nor did he devise plans to flee and escape execution. No, as we saw already, he used the time to pray. He knew that four people can accomplish more than one, so he quickly established a prayer circle. Four weak but believing men, four simple exiles from Judah went down on their knees and laid their predicament before God's throne. They wrestled with God and asked Him for the impossible.

Their major prayer request was not to receive some of God's wisdom, in order to, be able to *interpret* Nebuchadnezzar's dream. First, they would have to come up with the *con-

tent of the dream. With folded hands, they hoped to extract God's secret from Him. They did know by faith that nothing is impossible for God, and that therefore nothing is impossible for us if we truly believe. "I tell you solemnly, if your faith were the size of a mustard seed you could say to this mountain, 'Move up from here to there,' and it would move" (Matt. 17:20 JB). That same faith can command a dream to emerge from the dark recesses of the unknown, and it will do so.

Here the contrast between Nebuchadnezzar and Daniel, the world and the church, is complete. Nebuchadnezzar consults human wisdom when he gets into difficulty, but Daniel appeals to the wisdom above. When he seems to be trapped, Nebuchadnezzar turns to force and tries to fight his way out by decreeing that all the wise men must be put to death. But when Daniel sees no way out, he takes refuge in God and relies on the power of prayer. He knocks tirelessly at the gates of heaven.

Because of his unholy use of the power of the sword, Nebuchadnezzar became a *disintegrating* force within this state, for he proposed to rob the state of many of its most knowledgeable men. But Daniel, who relied on the holy power of prayer, became a *preserving* force for the land and the people. Because of his intervention, the lives of all those wise men were ultimately spared.

In his fear and rage, Nebuchadnezzar even tried to destroy his last hope, but Daniel, through his calm and confident prayer, made the impossible possible. God heard Daniel's appeal and disclosed his secret: "Then the mystery was revealed to Daniel in a vision of the night" (2:19). Daniel's prayer was answered by way of a night vision, a dream.

This reveals another aspect of the contrast between Daniel and Nebuchadnezzar. Earlier we saw that Nebuchadnezzar could no longer sleep because of his anxiety, but Daniel and his friends slept soundly after they had prayed. Faith made such sleep possible for them. Sometimes it can be sinful to sleep in the presence of Jesus, for example, in Gethsemane or in church. But there are also times when a believer *should* sleep. Daniel knew what it was to lie down at night and commend his spirit to God's care in the assurance that God would awaken him the following morning.

Peter later demonstrated the same strong faith. When Herod was about to behead him, he had to spend his last night in prison. Now, we might think that he would not be able to sleep at all, that he would pace around anxiously in his cell. But that's not how it actually went. "The very night when Herod was about to bring him out, Peter was sleeping between two soldiers, bound with two chains" (Acts 12:6).

Blessed are those who can sleep the way David, Daniel and Peter slept. But such sleep is not the privilege of only a few. All who *watch* and *pray* before they go to bed should be able to sleep soundly.

Prayer is an exquisite *privilege*, but it's also a great *task*. God has given us prayer as a talent. Anyone who puts this talent to work for him enters a domain of unlimited possibilities and is able to accomplish what the minds of the wise men and the bloody sword of Arioch could not accomplish together. What astounding possibilities and opportunities lie before us only if we will reach out for them in prayer! Only through prayer could the situation in Babylon be saved and the confusion be ended. Only prayer was able to save the wise men, who would surely have gone to their deaths otherwise.

Aren't there a lot of people who have lost their eternal lives because they neglected prayer? Isn't there a lot of confusion that we could dispel if only we would turn to prayer? Isn't there something odd about that gathering of friends at Daniels house? After all, we, too, get together with friends regularly. When we do, we talk about all the problems in the political arena and in the church. We talk and talk and talk. We're especially fond of complaining. Sometimes we even fool ourselves into thinking that we've had a "spiritual" conversation. But that's an illusion, of course, for the attitudes we bring to such a discussion are the very opposite of spiritual.

Why didn't we get together for a prayer meeting instead? A prayer meeting? Such things just aren't done!

My friend, the firmness of your declaration that such things aren't done, that people would think it very strange if we were to hold a prayer meeting, is proof that we are becoming more and more worldly. Because we are so busy talking, we pass up golden opportunities for prayer. We simply don't bother to "seek mercy of the God of heaven." We neglect the talent of prayer!

This is a talent we have all been given. We can't rely on the usual excuses and beg off on the grounds that we have no talent in this area. God gives all His children the ability to pray. Let's hope that when the great day comes, we will not be condemned as lazy servants who have buried the talents entrusted to them in the ground, for then even the little we have will be taken from us.

6

The Talent of Revelation

*Bring me in before the king, and I will show the
king the interpretation (2:24).*

JUST WHEN ALL OF BABYLON was in an uproar, Daniel saved the day. He did so not by his own strength but by making use of the power of prayer. Actually, it was a very simple matter. Daniel was really no different from you and me. Thus, we are capable of the same sort of accomplishments through prayer—as long as we really know how to pray. Through prayer weak human beings like you and I become recipients of divine power.

What happened when Daniel prayed? The hidden secrets of the king's dream were revealed to him: he was shown both the text and the interpretation.

> To thee, God of my fathers, I give thanks and praise,
> > for thou hast given me wisdom and power;
> thou hast now revealed to me what we asked,
> > and told us what the king is concerned to know
> (2:23 NEB).

Here again we see that those who have something will be given even more. Daniel already possessed the beautiful talent of prayer. That's what gave him the quiet confidence to go to sleep at a time when all the wise men of Babylon did not know where to hide from Arioch, the executioner.

Now that God had answered Daniel's prayer, He gave him another talent—the talent of *revelation*. Then things were made more difficult rather than easier for this praying prophet. When God answered Daniel's prayer, he favored him, but at the same time He gave him a task. Privilege and duty go together. We are to utilize the talents we are given. After Daniel was shown the smallest details of the king's dream, he was also to let the light of revelation shine on it.

Two things strike us immediately. First of all, Daniel does not show off his newly acquired knowledge or brag about it. He does not puff himself up and say, "What a wise man I am!" It's true that the wise men had failed miserably and were trapped in a hopeless quagmire, but Daniel did not heap scorn on those who are without the light of revelation. He knew all too well that the light had been *given* to him. Once we realize that talents are *gifts*, we know better than to brag about them. Instead, Daniel protects the wise men, for they simply didn't know any better. He tells Nebuchadnezzar: "No wise men, enchanters, magicians, or astrologers can show to the king the mystery which the king has asked" (2:27). Daniel is even humble enough to admit: "This secret has been revealed to me not because I am wise beyond all living men" (vs. 30 NEB). True knowledge does not make us puff ourselves with pride.

In the second place, we should note that the prophet quickly becomes aware that he now has a new *task*. God did not tell him the details of the king's dream as a secret to be shared with no one, as a story that might amuse him but was not to be discussed with anyone else. On the contrary, Daniel knew that he was called to be a bearer of the light of revelation, that he was to make known everywhere what the Lord had shown him—even in the palaces of the kings. God does not let us in on His holy secrets just so we can share them with a circle of friends. He wants everyone to learn of His plans and bask in His favor. His love is to be communicated and shared.

Therefore, the first thing Daniel did after getting up that morning and giving thanks to God was to rush to Arioch with an urgent message: "Bring me in before the king, and I will show the king the interpretation." Daniel did not do so only because of his desire to tell the king about the one true God, whose wisdom goes far beyond all human wisdom; there were also human lives at stake. Hence, before he asked to be brought before the king, he said to Arioch: "Do not put the wise men of Babylon to death" (2:24 NEB).

We, too, receive instruction from God's revelation (the Bible) about all sorts of topics of which other people—even wise men—are entirely ignorant. We have been given a lot of information about "the things to come." We could almost say that there will be no more surprises for us. It frightens us to hear of wars and rumors of wars, but we are not surprised. We know about it in advance. We no longer join in the world's vain dreams of a Humanistic kingdom of peace and harmony here on earth. We also know what will happen to us when this life draws to a close. There are wise and learned people who put a great question mark on the gravestone, but we put an exclamation mark there. Death is swallowed up in victory! It is a doorway to eternal life—or a passageway to eternal death. It all depends on whether you believe in Christ or not.

We know all these things with complete certainty. Yet, we can't *prove* them, just as the shepherd boy had no proof for the philosopher who came to him and promised him an apple if he could prove the existence of God. But the clever boy did have an answer ready. He pulled two apples out of his knapsack and said, "They're both for you if you can prove that God *doesn't* exist."

We can't prove anything either way. Our only proof is faith—a proof of things not seen. That's why faith represents reliable knowledge—even more reliable than the truth that 2 plus 2 equals 4.

God wants to make us wise for the sake of our salvation. But we must be careful not to become "wise guys." Sometimes we are so horribly and disgustingly proud! Instead of sympathizing with those who do not know what we know, we shrug our shoulders. We believe that being Reformed makes us superior to the rabble unacquainted with God's law. But who are we trying to fool? Since when are we "wise beyond all living men"? Have we forgotten where that knowledge of ours comes from? *God* has revealed it to us! How, then, can we be so proud and foolish as to pretend that we figured everything out for ourselves?

There's something else to consider, namely, the danger that we may inflate ourselves so much with our knowledge of "Reformed truths" that we forgot about doing with the revelation what God intends us to do.

Now, God did give us that revelation in part for our own sakes. It provides a light on our path so that we no longer have to stumble about in the darkness, tripping over all sorts of unseen obstacles. God did indeed share the secret of His salvation with His friends so that they could enjoy a hidden fellowship with Him. Yet we are not to keep this marvelous secret to ourselves. Those spiritual hogs who hoard God's revelation in order to enjoy its delights all by themselves should be ashamed. Daniel certainly didn't hide his holy secret in his own room; he trumpeted that secret forth before the king and his subjects. "Bring me in before the king, and I will show the king the interpretation"!

God gives us revelation as a talent. "When a lamp is lit, it is not put under a meal-tub, but on the lampstand, where it gives light to everyone in the house" (Matt. 5:15 NEB). The apostle Paul instructs us to hold the Word of life before others. There is no need to draw the curtains completely so that no ray of light penetrates the darkness of the night. In fact, we *may not* block off God's light, for the welfare and very lives of others are at stake. Millions of people are in danger of being lost because they have no knowledge. They have strayed from the straight and narrow path and gotten lost because they have no light to guide their steps. Our silence is one reason for their plight. Another reason is our failure to illuminate everything around us with our conduct and actions.

It is not that we have light in ourselves, of course. We should shed light just as the moon reflects light and points back to the sun as the source of its light. In just that way we should reflect the light of Christ and point back to Him. We look to both the sun and the moon for light. The sun is itself a source of light, well the moon gets its light from the sun. Hence Christ can claim that *He* is the light of the world and also say to His church, "*You* are the light of the world."

Heaven help us if we don't reflect the light of Christ, for we will then be judged lazy and worthless servants who have buried the talent of revelation in the ground. Despite all our knowledge and light, we will be cast into outer darkness! If we fathom all the mysteries but do not have the love to use our knowledge to win our neighbors for the Savior, we are as useless as a noisy gong or a clanging cymbal. Just as the Father sent Christ into the world, He now sends us.

Our message to this world is the truth that we need to be reminded of repeatedly ourselves: there must be room for Christ! In the final analysis, this is the text and meaning of Nebuchadnezzar's dream.

Nebuchadnezzar saw a huge statue. Its head was made of gold, its chest and arms of silver, its belly and thighs of bronze, and its legs of iron. This colossus rested on feet made of a mixture of iron and clay. Subsequent interpreters have argued at great length about the question just which kingdoms and empires this statue represents. Actually, there is no world power that it does *not* represent. It represents the great empires of all ages. The anti-Christian forces may take on different forms as time passes; they may appear in the form of gold, silver, bronze, iron, or clay. Yet in essence they remain the same. It's always the same principle at work, whether we face the shining gold of liberal Humanism or the might of the iron curtain.

This huge statue is shattered by a stone. That stone is Christ, the stone that the temple builders of this world rejected and refused to build upon. To the amazement of the onlookers, the stone grows until it reaches the size of a mountain. The kingdoms of this world will all be overwhelmed by our God and His Christ!

The stone did not come along simply to destroy everything in its path; it came to make room, to prepare a place for the Christ. In the world to come, then, there will be ample room for Christ. There will be one kingdom left—the Kingdom of heaven, in which heaven and earth are united. In that Kingdom there will be room for Christ! In all the confusion at the world's courts and among the nations, why isn't there someone who stands up and says, "We must take *Christ* into account"? Why doesn't someone stand up at the Security Council of the United Nations and say, "Don't forget to leave room for Christ, ladies and gentlemen, for otherwise all we have built will be smashed"?

We must also make room for Christ in our own lives. We may not just reserve a corner for Him somewhere; we must give Him everything. The stone grows and grows until it becomes a mountain that fills the entire earth. This mountain will also be a dominant presence in our lives if we join in the triumph in song that the kingdom of this world has been taken over by our God and His Christ.

7

Man's Empire and God's Kingdom

These men, your majesty, have taken no notice of your command; they do not serve your God, nor do they worship the golden image which you have set up (3:12 NEB).

NEBUCHADNEZZAR WAS NOW completely cured of the unrest that accompanied the frightening dream dealt with in the lengthy second chapter of Daniel. The Bible does not tell us whether the period of time between the dream of the shattered statue and the erection of the golden image on the plain of Dura was short or long.

Without any transitional comment, Daniel 3 begins abruptly with these words: "King Nebuchadnezzar made an image of gold, whose height was sixty cubits and its breadth six cubits." Apparently, the king had shaken off his fears and anxieties. Away with worrying and long faces! Let's not waste our time thinking about possible tragedies and frightening nightmares. Let's eat, drink, and be merry!

Why should a king waste his time worrying about nothing? After all, there wasn't a single cloud in the sky. Everything was going well: Nebuchadnezzar was annexing one country after another.

There was nothing whatsoever to be seen of the shattering of the statue in the dream, the statue whose golden head represented his own kingdom. In fact, the statue in the dream seems to have given him a grandiose idea: he would now make such a statue himself, even more beautiful than the one he had dreamed about. His statue would not only have a golden head, it would be made completely of gold.

This decision shows that Nebuchadnezzar wanted to forget not only what he had dreamed but also what he had *said*. As you recall, he had said to Daniel: "Your god is indeed God of gods and Lord over kings" (2:47 NEB). But who wants to be held to every statement or promise he has ever made? Nebuchadnezzar was not the first of the earth's powerful figures to repudiate an earlier declaration, nor would he be the last. When Nebuchadnezzar set up that statue on the plain of Dura, he completely retracted the declaration he had made. He now wanted to worship a power much greater than God, and he would make others worship it as well.

The Bible does not tell us whether this golden statue was meant to represent one of Babylon's gods or goddesses. It is entirely possible that Nebuchadnezzar had something else in mind. The statue was probably intended to symbolize Babylon's *power*. This colossal statue of 60 cubits by six cubits (approximately 30 metres high by three metres wide) was meant to represent the great power Nebuchadnezzar himself had acquired. When people saw it, they would be amazed—and then bow down. The name of the plain where this statue was erected also suggests such an interpretation, for *Dura* appears to mean *fortress*. Thus, it was the military might of Babylon that received symbolic expression here.

Now, we must not try to squeeze more out of this text than it actually contains. Yet I cannot help drawing this line that begins in Daniel through to the Book of Revelation, where the number six plays an important role as well. I think of the Antichrist, who also had a great statue made, and of the beast's number, which is 666.

There is a definite anti-Christian aim evident in Nebuchadnezzar's building of this statue, for he was not content once the statue was up: he also demanded that people pay it the honor due to a god. Whether we regard this honoring as worship of Babylon's military might or of the power of the state or of Nebuchadnezzar himself, it clearly represents the deification of a mere creature, which is an unmistakable characteristic of the Antichrist.

A great deal was done to maintain and promote this newly established worship of man. The measures are described for us extensively in the rest of the chapter.

In Jerusalem, hymns of praise raise *quietly* to God, but in Babylon the worship service involves ceremony, advertising and propaganda. To begin with, all the powerful people of Babylon were harked all together by the king: "Then he sent out a summons to assemble the satraps, prefects, viceroys, counselors, treasurers, judges, chief constables, and all governors of provinces" (3:2 NEB). Just who all these high officials were is far from clear. Let's just say that they were the generals and admirals and officers of the realm—the high and mighty of Babylon. We read that they "stood before the image that Nebuchadnezzar had set up" (3:3). No doubt they stood at attention. The flags were flying as all these powerful officials raised their arms in the prescribed salute.

At this massive gathering of Babylon's powerful officials in full dress uniform, the statue was "dedicated." Following the custom of that part of the world, the statue would have to be clothed and "fed"; it would have to be "made alive," so to speak, so that the people could worship it. Everything had to look "genuine." Translating this into twentieth century terms, we could say that at that moment the power of the Babylonian state became the focus of a state religion. Because the new religion was proclaimed, a great religious feast was held, and festive music was played.

Equally impressive as the collection of powerful officials was the variety of musical instruments used. We read that a herald proclaimed:

> Men of all peoples, nations, languages! This is required of you: the moment you hear the sound of the horn, pipe, lyre, harp, bagpipe or any other instrument, you must prostrate yourself and worship the golden statue erected by King Nebuchadnezzar. Those who do not prostrate themselves and worship shall immediately be thrown into the burning fiery furnace (3:4-6 JB).

The punishment was severe: those who transgressed this law would be consumed by flames!

Perhaps we can best think of this furnace as a sort of limekiln into which the victim would be thrown from above through a narrow opening. But just what this furnace looks like is not important. In the twentieth century we know all about death ovens and the technology of extermination. Our modern ovens are even hotter and more frightful than Nebuchadnezzar's machinery of death.

Now, this burning fiery furnace was *the* weak spot in Nebuchadnezzar's system. Everything in the empire he had built up was wondrous and beautiful—the huge golden statue on the plain of Dura, the impressive parades, the beating drums, the devotional music. Everything was well planned and organized! But Nebuchadnezzar knew all too well that not everyone would join in willingly and spontaneously. Thus, he had to take steps to make certain that every last citizen kneeled before the statue. That was the purpose of the fiery furnace. He would use intimidation and terror to make the stubborn ones go down on their knees. Nebuchadnezzar would rely on fear to get his way. As I said, this was the weak point in the system. It meant that his regime would decline as soon as fear of the authorities began to diminish.

The beauty of our religion, which appeals to our minds and hearts rather than our fears, is that it calls for *free obedience*. No one is forced into anything. Jesus *asks* us to come to Him. No one need remain with Jesus against his will. Serving God must be a labour of love and not a quest for the dollar. The commands of God are songs of hope that we sing in a foreign land. If we kneel down only out of fear of the great blazing fire that never dies out, the glory and beauty of our faith will be lost.

But Nebuchadnezzar's decrees were not hymns: they were commands, orders. The intended response was not love but abject submission. The worship he instituted was not a matter of voluntary consecration. Its basis was iron-fisted force. Here, in a few sober words, the prophet Daniel shows us the great contrast between God's Kingdom and man's empire, the Kingdom of the Spirit and the empire of force, the cross and the burning fiery furnace!

In contrast to all the beautiful things to be found in that Babylonian empire, there were also a few ugly things, for example, the secret police that kept a close eye on anything and anyone that might be considered dangerous to the state. "Therefore, at that time certain Chaldeans came forward and maliciously accused the Jews" (3:8).

At Daniel's request, Shadrach, Meshach, and Abednego had been placed over "the affairs of the province of Babylon" (2:49). Hence, they were part of the elite and were invited to the feast of dedication. (For some reason not revealed to us, Daniel himself was not present.) These three Jews broke the spell at the great feast. When everyone else kneeled in worship, they stubbornly remained standing. They would bow down to no one but God. The fear of the fiery furnace made everyone kneel, but the fear of the Lord kept them from kneeling.

Now, the secret police were not asleep on the job. It was not long before these Chaldeans appeared before the king to make accusations against the three Jews.

The use of the word *Chaldeans* and *Jews* is an indication that racial hatred was a factor here. Hatred of Jews is a very old phenomenon. But the element of jealousy should not be overlooked either. These Chaldeans complain to the king about "certain Jews" who had been appointed over "the affairs of the province of Babylon" (3:12). These Jews held very high positions in the government. That would never do!

But the most important thing is that the Chaldeans hated the *religion* of the three Jews. (Of course, there were many other Jews who did bow down to the statue; these three were the only ones who refused.) The accusation was made even sharper as the Chaldeans reported to Nebuchadnezzar: "They do not serve *your* gods." The king got the message. "Furious with rage, Nebuchadnezzar sent for Shadrach, Meshach and Abednego. The men were immediately brought before the king" (3:13 JB).

Man's empire stands completely opposed to God's Kingdom; they are antithetical in nature and aims. In the Kingdom of Nebuchadnezzar, there is no place for anyone who refuses to sing in the pagan choir because of his race or beliefs. But there is a place for those who kneel down because they are *forced* to. Such compliance can never lead to high offices, such as the office from which the three Jews were removed.

In the Kingdom of Christ, there is no room either for anyone who refuses to bow before the King of all ages. Yet race is not a factor: Chaldeans are just as welcome as Jews. In Christ there is neither Jew nor Greek, barbarian nor Scythian. The only thing that really counts is voluntary consecration. Anyone who kneels only because others kneel may indeed become an elder or deacon in the church or perhaps even a minister, but he will never take his place on one of those twelve thrones in heaven. He will be cast out as a useless servant, for the basic law of love in the Kingdom of God is that we are to obey God's commandments conscientiously and cheerfully, with our whole heart.

8

God's Festival of Sacrifice

*But I see four men loose, walking in the midst of the
fire, and they're not hurt; and the appearance of the
fourth is like a son of the gods (3:25).*

WHEN SHADRACH, MESHACH, and Abednego broke the spell at Nebuchadnezzar's worldly festival by refusing to bow down to his golden statue, they were tied up in their own clothes and thrown into the burning fiery furnace without as much as a hearing. Then the music of the lyre and the trigon on the plane of Dura was accompanied by the screams of the helpless victims in the executioner's furnace. Nebuchadnezzar's festival of dedication found a counterpart in the sacrificial festival of Christ's slaughtering lambs. It really did become a *festival* for the three men in the fiery furnace, as we shall soon see.

Nebuchadnezzar quickly discovered that it's not as easy to wipe out the church of the Lord as to snuff out the life of an unwanted animal. To his amazement he found that he had *four* men to deal with rather than three. Standing in the way was a mysterious fourth man who represented a higher, divine power. In awe, he said of this fourth man that he looked like a "son of the gods."

We know who this wonderful deliverer is—the angel of the Lord, who places an invincible heavenly guard around those who live by God's will. We are reminded here of the angel of the covenant, the man with whom Jacob wrestled, who now hurried to the side of Jacob's descendants. This angel is the prefiguration of the Son of man, our Lord Jesus Christ.

The appearance of this fourth man was doubtless an answer to the prayer of the three men in the fire. It is simply inconceivable that the three did not pray before they were thrown into the furnace. It was because they believed and had *already* prayed that they were able to say to the king: "our God whom we serve is able to deliver us from the burning fiery furnace; and he will deliver us out of your hand, O king" (3:17).

We do not actually read in the Bible that the three men prayed, for the Bible does not waste time relating superfluous or obvious details. Nor does the Bible tell us what they prayed. In the apocrypha, which is also instructive reading for Christians, we find something called "the prayer of Azariah" (or Abednego) includes these words:

> In all that you have done your justice is apparent:
> your promises are always faithfully fulfilled,
> your ways never deviate,
> your judgments are always true.
> You have given a just sentence
> in all the disasters you have brought down on us
> and on Jerusalem, the holy city of our ancestors,
> since it is for our sins that you have treated us like this,
> fairly as we deserve.
> Yes, we have sinned and committed a crime by deserting you,
> yes we have sinned gravely;
> we have not listened to the precepts of your Law,
> we have not observed them,
> we have not done what we were told to do
> for our own good.[2]

This prayer strikes me as authentic, for believers are always humble when they pray. They do not pretend to be wronged innocents but confessed straightforwardly, "*We* have sinned." Instead of pointing out the sins of others, they worry about their own sins. Azariah does not complain about the wickedness of Nebuchadnezzar or the evil world; instead, he laments his own sins and the sins of his people. If we look carefully and

---

2. The translation is taken from the *Jerusalem Bible*, where it is printed as Daniel 3:27-30.

honestly, we can always find the sins of the world in our own lives—even if only on a smaller scale.

When the whole empire kneeled before Nebuchadnezzar's majestic statue, Shadrach, Meshach, and Abednego were not astounded at the idolatry, for they recognized it as the same sin that the chosen people had engaged in when they kneeled before the Baals and the Astartes. We have lived ungodly lives! That's why we're in a fix now. Deal with us justly, Lord!

The presence of the angel of the covenant in the blazing fire shows us something of the light of Golgotha breaking through the darkness. The Son of God has seen us in the hellish fire of God's just judgments on our sins.

The fires of hell will never go out. Jesus descended into those flames to give us such complete, perfect salvation that the preservation of Daniel's three friends in the fire can only reflect it weakly, even though we are told that "the fire had no effect on their bodies: not a hair of their heads had been singed, their cloaks were not scorched, no smell of burning hung about them" (3:27/94 JB). The story of the fiery furnace and the fourth man who looked like a "son of the gods" is a prophecy pointing to Christ's descent into hell. Behold the Lamb of God who takes away the sins of the world!

The world held its festival of dedication on the plane of Dura. But in this world's vale of tears, God arranges His festival of sacrifice on the cross, as sacrifice that condemns us and cries out: "For God so loved the world that he gave his only Son, that whoever believes in him should not perish but have eternal life."

While the world rejoices to the music of the lyre and the trigon and sings in harmony as it kneels to worship the glory and power of man, the church lies prostrate before the cross and adoration of her Redeemer—the cross that is here being raised before its amazed eyes. There is a joyful sound in the tents of the believers, but it is not like the rich and intricate music on the plain of Dura. The song of God's people is the harmonious hymn of simple faith: "There is no condemnation for those who are united with Christ Jesus (Rom 8:1 NEB). Therefore, we may ask:

"O Death, where is your victory? O death, where is your sting?" (1 Cor, 15:55 NEB).

It is God alone whom we are to praise, for His glorious name is a source of great joy to us. Therefore, we must tell everyone about the wonders He has performed.

Just as all the officials and governors and counselors and members of the king's court crowded around the three men who emerged from the blazing furnace unharmed, eager to see for themselves whether their bodies and clothes had really been untouched by the fire, the work of Christ can be observed by looking at those whom He has redeemed. If I accept with a believing heart what Christ did for me, His work in me will be so complete that it will seem just as though I had never sinned but had achieved personally the perfect obedience that Christ performed in my place. In Christ, there is no outward glory, as there was in Nebuchadnezzar's statue. The cross casts a long shadow, and the flames spread their reddish glow.

The three men did not know in advance whether God would save them in the fiery furnace. If saving them would advance God's honor, He would surely do so, but they knew that they also had to reckon with the possibility of being consumed by the fire. Yet, even if they did perish, their death would serve to glorify God. The three men declared: "If our God, the one we serve, is able to save us from the burning fiery furnace and from your power, O king, he will save us; and even if he does not, then you must know, O king, that we will not serve your God or worship the statue you have erected" (3:17-18 JB).

In this story, death was swallowed up in victory. But we may not jump to the conclusion that no harm will ever come to us, or that God will spare us all hardship. No, we must prepare ourselves for the very opposite of a safe and secure existence! Because of the inner communication between Christ and His church, the church will always have to bear the cross. Christ warns us that we will be hated, just as He was hated.

In all eras of history, God lays His church on the altar as He celebrates His festival of sacrifice. There is *always* a furnace prepared for the church—the furnace in which bricks were made in Egypt, the fiery furnace on the plain of Dura, the stake at which martyrs have been burned throughout the church's history, the concentration camps behind the Iron Curtain.

One day, the second Nebuchadnezzar, the ultimate anti-Christian dictator, will set up his great statue and prepare a huge fiery furnace for the church in case she should refuse to honor his gods. When the believers are asked what has become of the God who is supposed to deliver them in their hour of peril, they will be able to answer in faith that whatever suffering they must endure in the present, they have a great destiny in store for them, for the day of salvation is dawning.

This is not to say that all of us will live to experience that day. Whether we do or not makes little difference, for our lives *today* must be characterized by the willingness to be sacrificed, to be thrown into the flames for Jesus' sake. Woe to anyone who does not know what the sacrifice of self-denial is, who does not know what it is to crucify the evil desires of the flesh and bury them, who does not feel called to devote himself in thankfulness to God as an offering of gratitude. Woe to the man unacquainted with the flames.

At the same time, a life governed by the cross is a life of *joy*. It might appear that all the joy and fun is on the plain of Dura, while the fiery furnace has nothing but intense, stifling heat to offer. But don't let appearances fool you. The citizens of Nebuchadnezzar's empire live in permanent fear, whereas we are happy and free under the rule of Christ—even if we find ourselves in the furnace.

In another of the apocryphal additions to the book of Daniel, we are presented with "the song of the three men in the fire." the song teaches us that it is possible to sing even in the most horrible circumstances:

> Cold and heat! Bless the Lord
> Give glory and eternal praise to him.
> Dews and sleet! Bless the Lord:
> give Glory and eternal praise to him.[3]

This is the glory of the church. The church knows how to rejoice in times of oppression because she knows that *sin*—rather than the intense heat of the furnace—is what makes life so somber.

Once we are delivered from sin, we are also delivered from anxiety and sadness. Then we will know what it means to rejoice at all times. The fire of the furnace did not consume the three men, but it did burn up the bonds restraining them, with the result that they were able to walk about freely. In this way, all things work together for our good. The flames do not spare us entirely. Yet, all they actually destroy is what needs to be destroyed and removed from our lives if those lives are to glorify God. To the extent that the flames consume wood is outward, we grow in purity and holiness day by day.

---

3. Daniel 3:67-8 in the *Jerusalem Bible*.

From this perspective we recognize that every sickness is a medicine, every loss a gain. Even death turns out to be a door leading to eternal life. The fiery furnace becomes a festival, a much greater celebration than the one held on the plain of Dura. Those are blest flames. "Fire and heat! bless the Lord: give glory in eternal praise to him." And you, my soul—you should praise Him most of all!

9

Nebuchadnezzar's Hallelujah

Nebuchadnezzar said, "Blessed be the God of Shadrach, Meschach, and Abednego (3:28).

THERE ARE ALL SORTS OF STRANGE things going on in the third chapter of Daniel. We already heard about the miracle of the three men emerging unharmed from the flames. But isn't the king's hallelujah, his "Blessed be God," with which the story of the golden statue on the plain of Dura ends, just as amazing? It's all the more astounding because it comes from the mouth of Nebuchadnezzar, the heathen dictator!

It comes from his *mouth,* but not—unfortunately—from his *heart.* Yet even so that triumph is great. The entire area around the golden statue was to be dedicated to the praise of human power: all lips were to declare, "glory be to man!" But now the one who organized and decreed all this idolatry says,

"Glory be to God!" The same man who had given the command that all nations were to kneel and worship before the statue suddenly changed his mind. Now he declared: "Men of all peoples, nations and languages! Let anyone speak disrespectfully of the God of Shadrach, Meshach, and Abednego, and I will have him torn limb from limb and his house razed to the ground, for there is no other God who can save like this" (3:29/96 JB).

We would never have suspected that this stately and impressive heathen festival of dedication would lead to such a conclusion. Especially when we saw the first three men thrown into the furnace, we were afraid. But God was heading toward this outcome from the very beginning. His name was to be glorified even on the plain of Dura.

The Lord used these three Jews as instruments to reach that goal and made them faithful unto death. These three men represented the *church* of that era. It was not a very large church numerically, but who cares about numbers? God's concern is not with numbers but with faithfulness. What great things are possible if only the church remains faithful!

Faithfulness changes everything. A heathen orgy of idolatry is suddenly transformed into a song of praise to God: "Blessed be the God of Shadrach, Meshach, and Abednego"! What I mean to say is this: in our world, which is so full of the deification and glorification of man, it's time for us to stop complaining. Instead, we should be ashamed. After all, what have *we* actually done about it?

But at the same time, I must emphasize that the Lord used these men as *instruments*. If they had tried to save themselves through human means, they would have failed, of course. But because Christ defends His church, hell is powerless to destroy it. That's how it was in Babylon, and that's still how it is today.

No doubt the greatest miracle of Daniel 3 is that there were people who did *not* kneel down and go along with the crowd, people who did not flee from the fiery furnace! That there was a church then and is a church now is not the result of our faithfulness or firmness of principle or any other quality of ours but is due to *Christ. He* sees to it that He is never without subjects. It is through *His* power that we are able to offer our lives as sacrifices of gratitude. That Christ brought all three men out of the flames unharmed is a miracle, and that the spirit of our time should fail to damage us is an equally great miracle.

The three Jews could certainly have found enough reasons to give in. We usually have little difficulty in silencing our consciences. Shadrach, Meshach, and Abednego were attending the festival as official representatives. Now, we all know that people in public life are forced to go along with various things that they would never approve of as private citizens and especially as Christians. What could be wrong, then, if they too were to bow? They wouldn't mean it anyway; it would be an empty ritual. If you complain about that, you're making a mountain out of a molehill. You're probably one of those people who are never satisfied!

Furthermore, the three men were given an opportunity to escape the punishment awaiting them. Nebuchadnezzar liked these three Jews. Apart from their rigidity in religious matters, they were capable men, men of whom he could make good use in governing his empire. These Jews were as honest as a summer day is long, which was something that Nebuchadnezzar could not say of many of his own people. Therefore, he wanted to be easy on them and leave the door open for them to change their minds.

Instead of taking the word of the Chaldean accusers, he asked: "Is it *true*, O Shadrach, Meshach, and Abednego, that you do not serve my gods or worship the golden image which I have set up?" (3:14). All they would have to say is that it was an oversight on their part, and the matter would have been forgotten. Should they deny their principles? Let's not forget that there was a task for them in Babylon.

Yes, there were enough excuses and avenues of escape available. We know how to handle such matters and make use of the standard defences. But the three Jews refused to budge from their position: "You must know, O king, that we will not serve your God or worship the statue you have erected" (3:18 JB). They didn't beat around the bush. The faithfulness expressed in these clear, concise, courageous words meant that the death sentence would have to be carried out.

Let's not jump to the conclusion that since such faithfulness unto death will probably not be required of us, we won't need the same kind of courage rooted in faith. Dying for the Lord requires faithfulness. But so does living for the Lord; it requires a faithfulness that must be apparent especially in little things, for faithfulness is a matter not of playing to the grandstand but of doing your duty mainly in life's obscure corners, where so often there is no one to watch you.

Faithfulness is needed especially on the night shift. I must emphasize this because it's so easy to go astray on this point. There's so much counterfeit currency in circulation. Sometimes we mistake being in a rut or acting out of mere habit for faithfulness. Anyone who calls attention to his faithfulness—whatever kind of faithfulness it may be—has already gone wrong, for faithfulness is not a manufactured item to be put on display at a fair to win the admiration of men.

The more we examine the events on the plain of Dura, the more contrasts we see between the Kingdom of God and Nebuchadnezzar's empire, between the church and the world. On the plain of Dura, we see the great and glorious statue, well before the three Jews we see the fiery furnace. The subjects of Nebuchadnezzar live under a regime based on force; they are governed through fear. Contrasted with this is a song of praise of three men in the fire, they are sorry for their sins, yet they are happy.

Alongside this double contrast, another contrast now becomes apparent. We see in these pious men a touching faithfulness completely foreign to the heathen Nebuchadnezzar. The king goes from one god to another. He worships any God that strikes his fancy. Now that the God of Shadrach, Meshach, and Abednego has done something amazing, he also makes a place for Him in his pantheon—only to renounce Him later and vilify Him.

That's why Nebuchadnezzar's hallelujah sounds so impure and hypocritical. He does say, "Blessed be God," but he does so not out of deep devotion but only out of self-interest. After all, who knows what advantages friendship with this God of the Jews might bring?

The worst thing is that what Nebuchadnezzar felt in his heart and what he did was not in harmony with what he said. Now, Nebuchadnezzar did indeed take some unusually stern measures: he decreed that anyone who spoke ill of the true God would be cut to pieces. But he never got around to the very first measure needed, namely, taking down the golden statue that dishonored God and smashing it to bits.

The statue remains standing on the plain of Dura. Sixty cubits high and six cubits wide, it glistened magnificently in the light of God's sun. It was at the foot of this unholy statue that Nebuchadnezzar sang his song of praise to God. Hallelujah! He was ready to destroy everybody and everything—except the lordly statue he erected.

Now we begin to see why Nebuchadnezzar's imperial hallelujah is suspect after all. Those are mere words, Nebuchadnezzar, and words are cheap. There would be no better way for you to honor God than by destroying that statue, but that's just what you won't do, you're ready to strike out at anyone who dares speak ill of God, but you don't get angry at yourself because of the blasphemous statue standing there untouched and undisturbed.

This is an old story, a story that has been repeated many times throughout history. In the New Testament we also read about such a king—Herod, who did a number of things after he heard John the Baptist preach but never got around to doing the one thing that needed doing most of all, namely, sending away his unlawful wife Herodias. There's nothing easier than shouting hallelujah, and there's nothing harder than smashing the statue on the plain of Dura.

Earlier I expressed my belief that Nebuchadnezzar was glorifying *himself* when he erected that golden statue. If I'm right, this would explain why doing away with the statue would be so difficult for him, for *self-glorification* is the very opposite of *self-denial*. It means saying to that sinful, proud, stubborn ego of mine: "I don't know you, and I don't want to make your acquaintance either. I want nothing to do with you. I would rather crucify you and bury you." It's much nicer and more pleasant to defend yourself and remain who you are—by leaving that glorious statue 60 cubits high and six cubits wide standing!

Yet, even as we do so, we sing, "Blessed be God!" shouldn't we be singing, "Praise the Lord, and honor His name"? Isn't that just the hymn for festive occasions, and shouldn't we go on to sing, "He heaps His favor on us day by day"? And if we like hymns, we could also sing, "Hallelujah, eternal honor and praise to God!" Isn't that a beautiful sentiment to express in a hymn? I would hate to think what might happen to those who cannot join in this hymn but speak ill of God instead. Didn't Nebuchadnezzar talk about cutting such people to pieces? Worse yet, didn't Jesus say something about a fire that will never go out?

What do you suppose will happen to us if we join Nebuchadnezzar in singing a new song to the Lord but continue following our old ways, making no effort to change? What will happen if the statue in your life—you know what it is—remains untouched and undisturbed and the image of Christ is not reflected in you? Remember that when Christ was vilified, He remained silent, and when He was made to suffer, He did not respond with threats.

Don't you realize how completely false that "Blessed be God" must sound in the ears of God and His angels? It doesn't just sound false; it sounds like a curse! Therefore, I need hardly point out that in the New Jerusalem there will be joyful singers only—and no one who sings out of tune. There will be no one there who does abominable things or other lies. In other words, there will be no room for anyone unwilling to change his way of life and unwilling to smash that accursed statue of his own ego on the plain of Dura as a first and continuing conversation deed. "Not everyone who says to me, 'Lord, Lord,' shall enter the Kingdom of heaven, but he who does the will of my Father who is in heaven" (Matt. 7:21).

"Blessed be the God of Shadrach, Meshach, and Abednego." This confession from the mouth of Nebuchadnezzar certainly has some value and meaning for this *earth,* for it meant that God's name was recorded in Babylon's archives. Moreover, it demonstrated clearly the importance of the idols. But such a confession has no value whatsoever for *heaven*.

Our fathers used to declare: "We believe in our hearts and confess with our mouths that there is an eternal and simple spiritual being that we call God, that He is incomprehensible, invisible, unchanging, infinite, omnipotent, completely wise, just, good, and an overflowing fountain of all good things." This confession contains much more than Nebuchadnezzar's hallelujah, for our fathers sealed it with their blood. Let's pray that *our* hearts and deeds may be in accord as well. Then we will truly be able to praise the Lord and shout our hallelujah.

10

Thou Art the Man!

*The tree which you saw grow and become strong,
reaching with its top to the sky, visible to the earth's
furthest bounds... that tree, O king, is you*
(4:20-2 NEB)

THE WHOLE SAD STORY OF Nebuchadnezzar's temporary madness, which was already foretold in the dream about the tree, is communicated to us in the scriptures within the framework of a royal proclamation: "Nebuchadnezzar the king, to men of all peoples, nations and languages, throughout the world: 'May peace be always with you. It is my pleasure to make known the signs and wonders with which the Most High God has favored me'" (3:31-2/4:1-2 JB). That's how this royal declaration begins. We hear the same tone at the end of the chapter: "Now I, Nebuchadnezzar, praise and extol and honor the King of heaven; for all his works are right and his ways are just; and those who walk in pride he is able to abase" (4:37).

These are not words to take lightly. If we don't know better, we might wonder whether Nebuchadnezzar was perhaps one of the Lord's prophets. But we have already seen how seriously we can take the hallelujahs of this tyrant. And when we take a careful look at his speech from the throne, it quickly becomes apparent that God's honor, which Nebuchadnezzar seemingly wants to proclaim, actually takes a back seat to his own interests. Of course, Nebuchadnezzar is not unique in this respect. Many who sing the Lord's praises and defend His name zealously and anxiously, "Did you hear what *I* said and see all that *I* have done for the Lord?"

Nebuchadnezzar makes a bad impression at the very outset by directing his proclamation to "men of all peoples, nations and languages, throughout the world." Look at *me*, Nebuchadnezzar, the world emperor! Apparently, the poor man has returned to his senses and no longer lives like an animal, but he has not yet been cured of his insane pride and his desire for self-glorification! Moreover, he cannot resist referring to Daniel as the one "who was named Belteshazzar after the name of my god" (4:8). Daniel had indeed interpreted his dream for him, but the vain king suggests that he was only able to do so because he bore the name of *Nebuchadnezzar's* god.

Finally, we must remember that Nebuchadnezzar's motives for making this imperial announcement were not religious but purely *political*. Naturally, everyone knew that Nebuchadnezzar had lost his mind and that he had been locked up for a while like a wild animal. No one, of course, wants to be governed by a ruler who is out of his mind: the king should be a wise man! Therefore, to dispel the mistrust and fear of his subjects, Nebuchadnezzar issued this proclamation. Anyone who read it would quickly realize that the king's mental health had been restored. Thus, the words sent out by Nebuchadnezzar in his eloquent decree were not the ravings of a madman. His intention was to publicize the fact that he had been fully healed.

What had happened to Nebuchadnezzar? What is the background of this proclamation?

The king had again been shaken up by a frightening dream. (It doesn't appear that the rich and powerful are able to sleep very well.) Since many of the things that crop up in a dream are matters that are on the dreamer's mind when he is awake, we may take that this dream, which was sent by God, gives us a look into Nebuchadnezzar's soul, revealing his most secret thoughts to us.

He dreamed that he saw a great tree, an immense tree that drew the attention of everyone and could be seen from any point on earth. The top of this tree reached all the way to heaven (4:11). Of course, this tree needed a great deal of "room" and soaked up the light and nourishment that the smaller trees around it also needed. But who would think of aggression and violence in connection with a tree? This tree is benevolent; its large branches provide shade for all the smaller creatures around it. It becomes the protector of the defenseless, as it were. "Its leaves were fair and its fruit abundant, and in it was food for all. The beasts of the field found shade under it, and the birds of the air dwelt in its branches, and all flesh was fed from it" (vs. 12).

That was the great dream of Nebuchadnezzar! He dreamed of a large, powerful state that would live and expand at the expense of other states, relying on force if need be. This state would let others go on living—but only as its dependence existing in its shadow!

God in heaven defends His rights when they are violated. Thus, a heavenly watchman gives the order to cut down the tree and cut off its branches. The stump and roots would not be destroyed, but the tree would be stripped of its foliage, its glory. It was also decreed: "Let a beast's heart be given him and seven times pass over him!" (4:13/16 JB).

I will come back to these details later. For the present it is clear not only that there is punishment in store for this tree but also that this punishment will be meted out to Nebuchadnezzar himself. After all, a tree has no heart, but a *person* does. And it is a person whose heart is to be changed into a beast's heart.

Nebuchadnezzar understood this immediately. Consequently, he wanted more details about the punishment hanging over his head. From a psychological standpoint we can understand why he turned first to the fortune tellers, magicians, astrologers, and Chaldeans, despite their lack of success in the past. On the one hand he wanted to put an end to the uncertainty, and on the other hand he was afraid to hear the truth. Whatever these soothsayers told the king, their answers apparently didn't satisfy him. Therefore, he had to turn to Daniel again (4:8).

God's prophets make no effort to disguise the truth. They know that only the *truth* can make us free. All the same, they are not people who take pleasure in announcing God's judgments. Although the king was indeed the oppressor of Daniel's people, there was no desire for revenge in Daniel's heart. He took no pleasure in the thought of the king's downfall. In fact, he was speechless for a whole hour because he was so upset when the meaning of the dream became clear to him.

When he finally did speak, he declared: "My lord, may the dream apply to your enemies, and its meaning to your foes!" (4:16/19 JB). That was Christ's spirit of love at work in Daniel. But love is never in conflict with the truth. Consequently, the faithful preacher Daniel hid nothing but told the king forthrightly: "That tree, O king, is you!" We are reminded of the occasion when the prophet Nathan said to David, "Thou art the man!"

This statement is the heart of all homiletics. Personal preaching speaks to the individual in the pew and does not spare the most secret sins. It shakes up even the most pious person in the audience. That kind of preaching keeps us from pointing our finger at our neighbor in the pew and shaking our heads about the wicked world out there. "Thou art the man!" Such preaching is also theodicy, for it explains God's ways to us.

Nebuchadnezzar's sin was overweening pride and imperialism. Therefore, he could not rightly protest against God's judgment. The man who exercised control over so many nations was now to lose control over his own mental faculties. This famous king was to be regarded by everyone as a beast. That was his punishment.

But this judgment was tempered with mercy. Every sinner, great or small, is given an opportunity to repent and humble himself. Nebuchadnezzar was given a stay of execution too. Daniel implored the king: "Redeem your sins by charity and your iniquities by *generosity to the wretched*" (4:27 NEB).

The italicized words show us Nebuchadnezzar's sin more clearly. He was guilty not only of the positive sin of using violence but also of the negative sin of failing to be gracious and merciful to the wretched of the earth. In Psalm 72 we read that Christ will rule the poor in a just, wise, and gentle way, and that He will give ear to their complaints. This gracious rule of Christ represents the norm for all human kings. The methods of violence, oppression and self-glorification used by the heathen dictator were *anti-Christian*. It was high time to repent of those sins and reflect something of the image of *Christ* by being gracious to the poor and wretched in his kingdom. The doctrine that rulers are God's servants applied to Nebuchadnezzar too. "By *me* kings reign, and rulers decree what is just" (Prov. 8:15).

Daniel 4 could well have been written for our time, for Nebuchadnezzar is not a figure from the grey past. Just think of the mighty trees in our time that leave no room for smaller trees but are concerned only with maintaining themselves—dictators and democrats, nationalists and imperialists, communists and capitalists, all the builders of world empires who do not cease from their iniquities just because someone talks about justice, even though they mouth the slogan themselves.

The frightening thing is that the sin of Nebuchadnezzar has even penetrated into the domain of the Kingdom of God, and that there is hardly a place in the arena of Christian education, the church, the family, and the Christian labour movement that has not been infected by it. Daniel's statement, "That tree, O king, is you" is addressed to all dictators, great and small—and there are many of them. Nebuchadnezzar's sin is also *our* sin!

We all remember what that sin was: not manifesting the image, the likeness of Christ in our lives. It is the anti-Christian evil of *self-glorification,* of proclaiming ourselves sovereign in all areas of life.

Christ did not seek to glorify Himself. Instead, He underwent humiliation and became the servant of all. Yet we Christians say, "*I* want my own way. *I* refuse to take a back seat. *I* want some recognition for what I've achieved." We all look out for ourselves, with little regard for others. We have already become large trees, but do we have enough room for further growth? Since we are trees with a heart—the heart of a beast?—and human arms, we'll use those elbows of ours to advantage. We'll see to it that we have even more room to grow and become strong—by pushing others aside!

But when God carried out His judgment on that piece of deadwood named Nebuchadnezzar, the king who refused to reflect the image of Christ in how he governed, what will he do with us, with the green wood? We know it all—we know it all too well. "Let this mind be in you, which was also in Christ Jesus" (Phil. 2:5 KJV). Therefore, Daniel points at each of us when he says, "Thou art the man!"

There is another pressing question that calls for an answer: How is Christ present in *your* life? Where do we see His image reflected in *your* conduct? God's wish, of course, is that we repent and live. Let's not forget what Daniel said to Nebuchadnezzar: "May it please the king to accept my advice: by virtuous actions break with your sins, break with your crimes by showing mercy to the poor, and so *live long and peacefully* (4:24/27 JB).

11

The Human Beast

The words were still on his lips, when a voice came down from heaven: "To you, king Nebuchadnezzar, the word is spoken: the Kingdom has passed from you. You are banished from the society of men and you shall live with the wild beast; you shall feed on grass like oxen, and seven times will pass over you until you have learned that the Most High is sovereign over the kingdom of men and gives it to whom he will" (4:31-2 NEB).

NEBUCHADNEZZAR WAS LITERALLY interrupted by God's judgment. While he was on the roof of his palace boasting and glorifying himself, he heard a voice from heaven announcing that he was to be punished. The king was cut off in the middle of his sentence, so to speak.

It's not as though he was not given sufficient warning. God had spoken to him privately, both in his dreams and when he was awake. Daniel had pleaded with him to break with his sins and rule justly. He was even given a year's stay of execution. But the king wanted to hear no more about it. He may have been awed by the dream at first, but when things went on just as before, the impression made by the dream quickly faded. Then he started dreaming wild, extravagant dreams that went far beyond the dream of the tree.

A year later he stood on the flat roof of his palace to get a good look at the monumental buildings he had constructed. That Babylon of his was indeed amazing! History has hardly seen anything comparable to it! The architecture bordering on the incredible. Nebuchadnezzar knelt in adoration before the God he worshipped above all others—his own ego. To the applause of hell, he brought himself a verbal offering of thanksgiving. "Was all of this not built by me alone?" he asked. Calmly and soberly the Bible declares: "The words were still on his lips, when a voice came down from heaven."

Of course! Not one of God's words is spoken in vain. Sin punishes itself. The insane pride of megalomania is punished with insanity. Nebuchadnezzar, the organizer and builder of a world empire, was doubtless a man of genius, but when almighty God makes His judgments known from heaven, the brain of the genius is clouded with madness.

Because he became a lunatic, Nebuchadnezzar was expelled from human company. In those days there were no hospitals for the mentally ill. As dangerous, unpredictable individuals, they were simply forced out of human society. All alone, Nebuchadnezzar lived as an animal. In our time, too, there have been cases of people believing themselves to be animals. The Bible gives us a description of this horrible condition: we read that Nebuchadnezzar "ate grass like an ox, and his body was wet with the dew of heaven till his hair grew as long as eagles' feathers, and his nails were like birds' claws" (4:33).

The mighty king to whom the entire earth had once bowed down was now seen moving about on his hands and knees. With his claw-like hands, he tore grass from the ground to feed himself. This went on day in, day out, for seven horrible "times" (presumably years), until no one could tell whether that miserable creature was really a man or an animal. He still had human eyes, but his behavior was that of a beast. Just as the dream had foretold, he was given the *heart* of a beast. There was nothing royal about him any longer. He had attempted to take the great leap forward to become "like God," but he had fallen flat on his face. The bigger they are, the harder they fall!

We have already learned this lesson from the Paradise story. Nebuchadnezzar, whose sin was that he did not want to manifest the image of God by establishing justice and righteousness in his kingdom, now discovered to his shame that he had been reduced to a caricature of a human being, a human beast, a monster, a madman!

Not only does Nebuchadnezzar's story point back to Paradise, it points ahead to our modern era. A book could well be written about our times under the title "It's a Mad, Mad World." Never has there been so much boasting about man's great achievements and empires, and never have there been such insane wars to destroy everything built up so painstakingly. It's hard to tell whether the beast or the genius has the upper hand in modern man. And what he invents and builds, man shows himself to be a genius, but his creative hands quickly grow fingernails like birds' claws once the desire to destroy others with all those modern inventions is born in his beastly heart. Modern man invents missiles to track down his prey as relentlessly as the eagle.

We call this modern civilization—people with claw like hands and kings with eagles' talons! The powerful rulers of this earth and all their counselors with them seem two have lost their minds completely. Devastating weapons of destruction are hidden by the hundreds and thousands all over the world, ready to explode at the push of a button. Many of the people in this insane world seemed to have the hearts of beasts.

But this isn't the end yet! Nebuchadnezzar's insanity may be revived in our time in a thousand different forms, for what we read about him in Daniel is only a weak reflection of what the horrified world will experience under the devilish rule of that great world dictator the Antichrist.

The world continues to dream of progress. Man's better instincts will win out in the end! A golden age will dawn as the beastly side of man, the part of him that makes him aggressive, is rooted out completely. Brotherhood will flourish on the renewed earth. There will no longer be wars to terrify us, since human egoism will vanish when no one is interested in wealth any longer and no one is in need. Such is the beautiful dream of the Humanist.

But the truth of the matter is that events in our world are moving in just the opposite direction. Instead of the moral superman, we see the human beast. The Cold War that began not long after the Second World War is not a prelude to a universal kingdom of peace. Instead, it prepares the way for the world dictator whose name is Antichrist. The Book of Revelation describes him as a great genius who will succeed in uniting the entire world around him in admiration.

John portrays the Antichrist as a beast rising out of the sea—the ever-turbulent sea of nations. The highest thing human culture can give birth to is the human beast, in who madness reaches its tragic culmination. This human beast is possessed by the insanity of the devil. This is the inevitable course of world history. We see the overall flow of events reflected in miniature in the story of Nebuchadnezzar, the king who became a beast!

We must not stare ourselves blind at Nebuchadnezzar and the wicked world, however, for if we do, we will surely forget another important question that needs to be asked: What does the word of God say to *me* here? In light of this question, the story of Nebuchadnezzar becomes a moving plea to seek communion with Christ—every day. Only through communion with Christ can our hatred of God and neighbor, the hatred that makes us resemble the beast, be overcome, and rooted out. Christ did not come into the world to carry us off to heaven after this life; He came first of all to put a stop to the devil's work and—to put it in positive terms—to restore God's image in us.

As soon as Christ became operative in our lives, we find it impossible to go on glorifying ourselves. Then begins general renewal in our lives. We are sanctified and made kings. Through Christ's power, the unholy sinner becomes a child of God and a child of the light. We learn to break with our sins and live righteously. We begin to atone for our iniquities by being merciful to the poor and wretched. Thereby we manifest the image of our King, Jesus Christ, who cares for the poor and gives ear to their complaint. In Jesus Christ alone is life, but apart from Christ there is only death!

Anyone who possesses the form of godliness but not its power, that is, anyone who gives sin a free hand in his life instead of letting Christ rule, will discover that sin is degrading his life in even greater measure. He will be unable to arrest the process of degeneration. The king turns into a beast. There's no getting around it: anyone who sins becomes a slave to sin!

It may be that little of this can be seen outwardly. In the eyes of men, we may enjoy high esteem—and perhaps in our own eyes as well. We may be thought of as godly people, just as though we were actually fighting in the front lines. Perhaps we may even become office bearers in the church.

Man can only see outward things, but the Lord observes what goes on in the heart. When the Lord affords us a peek into the depths of our own hearts, when the spirit of God drives us out of our self-imposed blindness, we are led to confess that we, too, have acted like beasts toward God.

Every one of us should pray for divine enlightenment, for the Bible also speaks in a chilling way of a resurrection of the dead to eternal horror; it speaks of people who will take on a frightful appearance even more revolting than the human beast Nebuchadnezzar with his hair as long as eagles' feathers and his nails like birds' claws. Such people will gnash their teeth in everlasting frenzy because their repentance came too late.

That's why we should take the story of Nebuchadnezzar as a fiery plea from the Holy Spirit to seek communion with Christ. Contrasted with the ugliness of the anti-Christian Nebuchadnezzar, the incomparable beauty of Christ shines through even more.

12

Multiplied Peace

*King Nebuchadnezzar to all peoples, nations, and
languages, that dwell in all the earth: peace be
multiplied to you! (4:1).*

THE BEGINNING OF THE ROYAL proclamation almost sounds apostolic: "Peace be multiplied to you!" the apostles often begin their letters with such words. But there's a world of difference, of course. Nebuchadnezzar is speaking only of earthly peace and prosperity, the kind of peace the world gives. This worldly dictator knows nothing of peace that passes all understanding.

Nebuchadnezzar's situation, which speaks of peace is highly paradoxical and leaves us with an unpleasant aftertaste. At first, it's sweet in the mouth, but it turns bitter in the stomach.

You can't help but laugh when you hear this tyrant Nebuchadnezzar, whose armies have subdued "all peoples, nations, and languages, that dwell in all the earth," speak here of peace. He speaks words of peace to his poor victims, who don't dare utter a sound or raise a finger against him. Actually, peace is secondary for Nebuchadnezzar anyway. The emphasis at the beginning of this proclamation falls not on the word *peace* but on "all peoples, nations, and languages." The king again draws himself up to his full height. Look at *me*, the ruler of the entire world! He says, "peace be unto you," but he means, "to me be the glory!" This powerful, worldly ruler certainly did not mean what the servants of Jesus Christ mean when they open a letter by speaking of peace as they bring the message of the blood of the cross.

This iron dictator, then wishes his subjected peoples peace. He is in the best of moods, for he is now completely healed of his dreadful insanity. The human being buried in the beast has re-emerged, and the king has regained his imperial glory: "At the moment my reason returned, and to the glory of my royal state, my majesty and splendor returned too. My counselors and noblemen acclaimed me; I was restored to my throne, and to my past greatness even more was added" (4:33/36 JB). Thus, a few benevolent words from Nebuchadnezzar to his subjects were certainly in order.

And you must admit that when this king is in a good mood, he speaks in magnanimous terms. "Peace be *multiplied* to you!" There are two ways of making a number greater—addition and multiplication. The first goes very slowly, but the second advances by leaps and bounds. 2 plus 2 equals 4, but 4 times 4 equals 16. Addition is the method of average man, where as multiplication is the method of kings. Kings don't do things on a small scale— "Peace be *multiplied* to you!"

Before I say anything more about this peace, let me return to the story itself. Earlier we saw that the Lord had not destroyed Nebuchadnezzar completely. In his dream a heavenly messenger has declared that the branches of the tree (Nebuchadnezzar) would be cut off, but the stump would remain rooted in the earth (4:15). Thus, the judgment was not absolute: Nebuchadnezzar would not be completely wiped out. The king would even be restored to his former state of glory as soon as he confessed "that the Most High is sovereign over the kingdom of men and gives it to whom he will" (vs. 32 NEB). This is just what happened, after the "seven times" had passed. One might be inclined to think of these "seven times" as weeks or months, but it is my belief that the king's mental illness lasted for seven *years*.

After his recovery, Nebuchadnezzar sent a manifesto to his people, which is reproduced for us literally in the fourth chapter of Daniel. One of the indications that we have an exact copy of the king's proclamation is the alternation between the first and third persons when Nebuchadnezzar speaks of himself. He begins the proclamation by using the first person. "It is *my* pleasure to recount the signs and marvels," he declares (4:2 NEB). "*I*, Nebuchadnezzar, was living peacefully at home in the luxury of my palace. As I lay on my bed, I saw a dream," and so forth (4:4-5 NEB). The conclusion of the proclamation is also written in the first person: "At the end of the appointed time, I, Nebuchadnezzar, raised my eyes to heaven and I returned to my right mind" (4:34 NEB). But in the middle section of the proclamation, Nebuchadnezzar speaks of himself in the third person, as though he were telling a story about someone else: "The words were immediately fulfilled: Nebuchadnezzar was driven from human society and fed on grass (4:30/33 JB). This is correct from a psychological standpoint! The episode of Nebuchadnezzar's animal existence had, in fact, taken place outside his human stream of consciousness. At that time the king was no longer himself. He was literally *out of his mind:* he was a stranger to himself!

This chapter ends with Nebuchadnezzar's word of praise for God. The Babylonian king glorifies the King of heaven and instructs his subjects to do the same.

Yet we must not regard this as a genuine conversion to God. We saw earlier that the proclamation was actually intended by Nebuchadnezzar as self-glorification. In addition, we discover that it is permeated by heathen ideas.

This is apparent from all sorts of details, including the way Nebuchadnezzar describes the appearance of the heavenly messenger who came to pronounce judgment on the great tree. Nebuchadnezzar reports that the messenger declared: "The sentence is by the decree of the watchers, the decision by the word of the holy ones" (4:17). According to his heathen understanding of the world, the destiny of men is determined by a council of extra-terrestrial beings, who are here called "watchers" or "holy ones." Apparently, Nebuchadnezzar was convinced that the decision about him had been made by this council of the gods, despite the fact that Daniel had earlier corrected him on this point by declaring: "It is a decree of the Most High, which has come upon my Lord the king" (vs. 24).

In light of Nebuchadnezzar's unyielding alliance to his own heathen way of thinking, we see that his praise of God cannot be taken at face value. In essence it represents an attempt to place the God of heaven in the heathen temple's collection of gods.

Even though we are faced here with the wonderful and amazing fact that the name of the Lord is inscribed in the official records of the Babylonian empire and stored in state archives, these words of praise to God do not really appeal to us. Those who worship the Lord must do so in spirit and truth; otherwise, their prayer becomes a curse.

More important is the fact that God used the healing of Nebuchadnezzar to maintain the peace of the gigantic Babylonian empire, and thereby the peace of the world. This is the same peace mentioned at the beginning of the royal proclamation and referred to by Daniel when he begged the king to repent and turn to God "that there may perhaps be a lengthening of your tranquility" (4:27). Thus, there is a clear connection between the healing of Nebuchadnezzar and the peace of the kingdom.

If Nebuchadnezzar had remained insane and this finally became clear to all the subject peoples of the empire, then "all peoples, nations, and languages" would have considered it time to finally throw off the hated yoke of the Babylonians. The result would have been worldwide revolution, chaos!

But God did not want chaos throughout the world at that time—not because He wanted to spare Nebuchadnezzar but for other reasons of his own! God was preparing the way for Christ; He was trying to open a path for the Kingdom of heaven. But He could not use chaos for that end. Therefore, he allowed Nebuchadnezzar to be healed, so that he could send swift messengers to all parts of the world and announce to the nations: "Peace be multiplied to you!" In that way, too, God was preparing for the heavenly messengers who were to announce a different kind of "peace on earth" one day in Bethlehem, a peace that would be to all people.

The dictatorial letter of Nebuchadnezzar prepared the way for the apostolic letters that declare: "May grace and peace be multiplied to you" (I Pet. 1:2). *Babylon's* herald of false peace served only to prepare the way for *Jerusalem's* heralds of true peace, who proclaimed to all peoples, nations, and languages the peace made possible through the blood of the cross. Nebuchadnezzar's kingdom of peace, in which all nations and languages were *compelled* to sing the praise of the emperor, is subordinated to the purpose of the eternal Kingdom of peace in which all nations and languages join as one voice singing the joyful song of the Lamb.

This also shows us how *we* should look at the question of war and peace. The whole world yearns for peace. Everyone longs to hear the chimes proclaiming peace and jubilant declaration, "peace be multiplied to you!" We, too, may wish and hope for peace—but only under a certain condition, namely, that the "world's peace" serves to promote the coming of Jesus Christ's eternal Kingdom of peace.

But if God has decreed that this Kingdom of peace must come through chaos and world revolution, through wars and rumors of wars, through the blood and tears of God's church, then we must hold our heads high in the knowledge that deliverance is at hand. The church has never dreamed of a peace on earth that would last forever or of a complete elimination of evil in this life. She looks forward to a new heaven and a new earth, where righteousness will dwell, and peace will literally be multiplied!

On the great and glorious day of the Lord, all the earth's powerful figures—like Nebuchadnezzar in this chapter—will glorify the King of heaven. *Every* knee shall bow to Him, and *every* tongue confess His name! This is not the same as being *forced* to utter words of praise. We will praise Him before His footstool, or sitting on the twelve thrones of Israel.

To be granted this privilege, it is not enough to enjoy the grace of God showed to Nebuchadnezzar when He gave him back his health and then restored peace in his kingdom. Yet, that's the kind of grace we have on our minds most of the time: we want health, prosperity, abundance, peace! We say to ourselves, "I will tear down my old barns and build new, larger barns to hold all the crops I have grown." But God intervenes and says, "You fool! Tonight, I will require your soul of you. What good will all your possessions do you then?"

Is there anyone reading these words who is at peace with himself without being at peace *with God*, without enjoying the peace of the cross? The amazing thing about this true peace is that it is *multiplied*. The father God leads us, the more we enjoy His presence.

When this peace descends on us, it descends on our neighbors as well. Those who are at peace with God become *peacemakers* among men. Blessed are the peacemakers, for they shall inherit the earth!

13

What Belshazzar Forgot

You have given no glory to the God who holds your breath and all your fortunes in his hands (5:23 JB).

THE STORY OF DANIEL 5 could be summarized as follows. King Belshazzar, the grandson of king Nebuchadnezzar, had arranged a great feast to which the most important gentlemen in Babylon were invited with their ladies. On this occasion he made use of the holy vessels which Nebuchadnezzar had taken from the temple in Jerusalem (1:2). When the boisterous delight of the revilers was reaching its peak, a mysterious hand suddenly appeared on the wall of the chamber where the banquet was being held and wrote a few words. The wise men could not read those words, but Daniel was able to read and explain them. The horrible correctness of Daniel's explanation was soon borne out: "That very night Belshazzar the Chaldean king was slain" (5:30).

It won't get us anywhere to dismiss this episode as a story about the gray and distant past, an interesting chapter of world history that we read with mixed emotions. What we need to do instead is to draw this story into the horizon of the present and discover—for there are many who need to learn this lesson—that in those fancy, decorated Bibles with which we are so familiar, God has written His blazing message in His own handwriting, a handwriting that cannot be read by today's wise men and intellectuals.

What Daniel said to Belshazzar also applies to us: "You know all this." We knew it, alright! Yes, we knew it from the time we were children. But we do not like being reminded that simple forgetfulness, a trivial sin of omission like the one in Daniel's indictment of Belshazzar, could lead to the death penalty. What was Belshazzar's sin? "You have given no glory to the God who holds your breath and all your fortunes in his hands."

Between the royal proclamation in which Nebuchadnezzar expressed his respect for the Most High and the story that concerns us now, about 30 years passed. A number of things had changed during that time. Nebuchadnezzar had died, and the crown of his world empire had passed on to Belshazzar. This chapter might leave us thinking that Belshazzar was Nebuchadnezzar's son, but that was not the case. It appears that he was his grandson. The queen, whom we will see appearing on the stage shortly, seems to possess the kind of authority and hold the kind of influential position that a "queen mother" would have at a court in the ancient Near East. Therefore, we are probably justified in supposing that she was not Belshazzar's wife but his mother—and a daughter of Nebuchadnezzar. From time to time she does speak of "King Nebuchadnezzar, your father," but in that part of the world there was nothing unusual about calling a grandfather a "father." The Pharisees, as you recall, like to speak of Abraham as their "father." Furthermore, it is apparent from the words of this "queen" that she was living in the past and was well acquainted with history, which also suggests that she was the mother of Belshazzar.

A second change, which is definitely a change for the worse, is that the prophet Daniel had apparently fallen into disfavor. He lived somewhere in Babylon as a forgotten citizen. Belshazzar didn't even know him! Now, Daniel was the bearer of the Word of God. Thus, as long as he had a position at the court, the Word of God made certain demands on life at the court. Daniel's presence meant that there was a continual recognition—even if it was only external—of the Most High God. But Daniel had been forgotten, and we all know how things go when the Word of God is shoved into an obscure corner. The water then breaks through the dam, and the river of sin overflows its banks. That's just how it goes in our own lives when we seek to escape the sound of God's Word. And the danger was all the greater at the heathen court of Belshazzar.

We already smell the stench of sin in the opening words of Daniel 5:

> Belshazzar the king gave a banquet for a thousand of his nobles and was drinking wine in the presence of the thousand. Warmed by the wine, he gave orders to fetch the vessels of gold and silver which his father Nebuchadnezzar had taken from the sanctuary at Jerusalem, that he and his nobles, his concubines and his courtesans, might drink from them. They drank wine and praised the gods of gold and silver, of bronze and iron, and of wood and stone (5:1-2, 4 NEB).

The timing of this drunken banquet was offensive in itself. Babylon was at war. Nabonidus, Belshazzar's father, was leading the troops. The land was in great peril, and the soldiers of Babylon were already staggering on the brink of defeat. As the soldiers on the battlefield were dying for king and country, as the widows were mourning, the frivolous playboy was holding a banquet in the palace for a thousand of his lords and drinking wine with his wives and concubines. Those powerful lords were cowards who would let others do the fighting when the critical movement arrived.

But even more horrible is what actually happened at the banquet. In Babylon, wedding celebrations and parties did not take place without any mention of a higher power, as so often happens in our society. On the contrary, religion was central to the celebration. (Doesn't that put us to shame?) No wine was consumed, and no glass raised until a song of praise to some deity was sung first. Bearing in mind the nothingness of these gods, the author of the book of Daniel tells us ironically: "They drank wine and praised the gods of gold and silver, bronze, iron, wood, and stone" (5:4).

At some point Belshazzar certainly hit upon the idea of using the holy temple vessels from Jerusalem at this drunken banquet. Wouldn't that be fun? He could drink sacrificial wine to his gods from the holy vessels stolen from the House of God!

What a horrible thought! We might compare it to a group of drunks stealing the church's communion set in order to drink from its glasses at their favorite bar. It's a wonder that Belshazzar and the other revilers didn't choke on the wine, that no one was struck dead.

God finally responded to this outrage. He answered by way of a trick that the revilers hadn't expected to see performed that night. They were not at all prepared for it. But that was of no concern to God, who so often shatters the mood at worldly festivals!

Most striking of all was the way God upset the revilers and made their hearts beat faster in fear. He did not bear His mighty *arm* to smash those who mocked Him. He didn't even intervene with his *hand*. He used no more than a few fingers on one hand. But a single *finger* of God can cause unspeakable destruction. This the Egyptians recognized when their wise men explained the plagues by declaring that they were the work of God's finger.

What did those fingers do in that palace? All they did was write a few words on the bare wall: "Suddenly there appeared the fingers of a human handwriting on the plaster of the palace wall" (5:5 NEB).

How powerful God is—even when He does nothing more than write! A wave of fear surged through the crowd. The king, in particular, was dumbfounded by what he saw. His entire face changed; he turned white as a sheet. He wanted to stand up, but his legs failed him. It was as though the shock had paralyzed him. The assembled lords were no braver; they were completely terrified by those few words written by the finger of God. Yet, their fright was not a healthy fear that would bring them to repentance.

Throughout the ages, it has been clear what God can accomplish just by writing a few lines. We all know that God wrote a great deal more than those few words on the palace wall: He wrote through inspired prophets and apostles who took pen in hand. The words in our Bible were written by the same hand as the words on Belshazzar's wall.

God's writing has brought about some amazing things in

human history. Innumerable sinners have been all but frightened to death by what He has written. They were so frightened that they no longer saw any way out but to turn to Jesus. What God has written in the Bible has blazed a path through history. Here, there and everywhere, people who were living in sin caught fire—but they merged from the flames renewed and purified. Through the Scriptures, God has changed the world.

And what about us? Is it perhaps because we are familiar with the scriptures from childhood on, because we have grown so used to the Bible, that its words of judgment no longer frighten us when we come across such stories as that of Belshazzar? Is it because of our familiarity with the Bible that we no longer see anything surprising in it, that we no longer recognize God's fingers?

Just think of all we do with the Bible. We read it from Genesis to Revelation. We explain the Scriptures, comment on them, and debate their meaning. We write longer and shorter scholarly works on the various books of the Bible and even produce paraphrases. We derive principles from the Bible and base our scholarship squarely on the authority of Scripture. The Bible contains no mysteries for us, as it did for the wise men of Babylon. Quickly and easily, we run through chapter after chapter.

But there is one thing we no longer do—tremble at the Scriptures! Is there anyone among us who is truly frightened at what he reads there, so that his whole face changes colour and his legs buckle under him?

For Belshazzar, it was the first time he had encountered God's writing. Belshazzar, if only you had some training in Biblical scholarship, you would never react in such a childish way! You have to get used to the language of the Bible!

Thus, we would do well to take the Scriptures a bit more seriously. King Belshazzar was warned that those who desecrate God's holy vessels will not escape punishment. In fact, it is not necessary to remove God's holy vessels from the temple and use them in a drunken fit of debauchery in order to desecrate them. That horrible possibility exists even *within* Jerusalem, *within* the church. We become guilty of this sin when we participate in a communion service with wrath in our hearts. We do so when we defile ourselves through illicit sex (Didn't you know that your body is a temple of the Holy Spirit?). No, let's not be too quick to point the finger at that rascal Belshazzar!

At the end of Daniel's indictment, we find the main thing he has against the king: "You have given *no glory* to the God who holds your breath in His hands." Belshazzar had forgotten to do that. Now, this was only a sin of omission! But it appears that such a sin is no less serious than desecrating holy vessels from the temple. Glorifying God is the purpose of every creature, from the highest to the lowest. Anyone who fails to glorify God has not responded to his calling and has not understood the meaning of his life. Any life of which it must be said that it was not God-glorifying is a miserable failure!

It's certainly a sobering thought that such an omission is regarded as a capital offence, for we don't accuse ourselves of this sin very often! We sometimes worry about certain evil deeds we have done, but our failure to glorify God doesn't concern us very often. We speak of a life well spent when we hear that someone has worked hard for his business and his family and has left a tidy sum to his heirs, or that someone has accomplished something for society or science. Much is made of this at the graveside, and the newspapers are full of it. Yet, if God was not glorified in that life, the God who holds all our breath in His hands, that "well spent" life will turn out to be completely and absolutely useless after all. It may even happen that someone who has been a "pillar" of the church is ultimately informed by God, "You have given Me no glory but have glorified yourself instead." Self-glorification has not died out by any means!

We should give this possibility our careful attention and stop to ask ourselves what our lives are really all about. Every evening we should review the events of the day to see whether we have glorified God. Of course, this glorification of God leads to certain consequences, just as the two sides of a balance scale affect each other: the higher one side goes, the lower the other side sinks. "He must increase, but I must decrease."

Oversight and forgetfulness can cost us our lives. A single man who causes a train accident by not paying attention to his duties is less guilty than a Christian who forgets that glorifying God is the primary purpose of his existence. When the last judgment comes, some will be cast into outer darkness because of seemingly small oversights: "I was hungry, but you did *not* feed Me."

14

What God Did Not Forget

The writing reads: Mene, Mene, Tekel and Parsin (5:25 JB).

BELSHAZZAR HAD COMPLETELY forgotten to give glory to God, in whose hands his fate rested, but God had *not* forgotten to pay careful attention to everything this royal scoundrel did. The Lord looks down from heaven and sees all the children of men. The last page of the book of Belshazzar's life was now laid open before his frightened eyes. Instead of "The End," which is what one would normally expect to read on the last page, God wrote His "Mene, Tekel" on the palace wall.

These words, of course, were meant as a warning. God is not out to destroy anyone's life without first giving him a fair warning. Even if someone is such a great sinner as to profane the holy vessels, even if the clock of his life reads five minutes before midnight, he still has time to repent.

Time had not yet run out for Belshazzar, for God's fingers were still writing. But woe to you when those fingers have finished writing! This same night your soul will be required of you, Belshazzar, king of the Chaldeans! Who will enjoy your kingdom and all your possessions then?

In addition to the written word, *history* had a lesson for Belshazzar. Both Scripture and God's revelation in history contained a message for the king.

What did history have to do with this matter? In the first place, the scholars of Babylon were called in to read the hieroglyphics on the wall, but they got nowhere. They could not read the words, nor could they interpret them. Once more human scholarship failed. They tried all sorts of things. They read words backwards and forwards. They pondered all the possibilities. They focused all their ingenuity and cleverness on those few simple letters, but they could not come up with a reading that held water.

Despite their efforts, the words on the wall remained an unsolved puzzle. After all, what could heathen scholarship make of something that God Himself had written? What is revealed to believing children remains a complete mystery to the wise men of this world! What the simplest messenger in the church can read and understand remains a dark mystery to the secular academy! Call those robed men and learned minds together; they will pull faces and scratch their heads and mumble big words, but in the final analysis they will get nowhere!

The failure of the scholars made the confusion and fear in the king's palace even greater. Finally, the clamor drew the attention of the "queen." History then entered the chamber again—this time in the awesome figure of the old queen mother.

The voice of history is often instructive. No one can neglect history's lessons and remain unashamed and unpunished! In the stern words of this old woman, we hear a subtle reproach directed towards the playboy who would rather throw parties than concern himself with the history and welfare of his land and people.

Three times the queen mother reminded Belshazzar about his "father." Now, Nebuchadnezzar was by no means the finest person who had ever lived. Furthermore, we must always be on guard against the temptation to attach too much of an aura of sanctity to our forefathers. Not all the deeds and words of previous generations can serve as reliable norms for us to live by. Only the Word of the Lord is a completely trustworthy norm for our life.

Now, this Word of the Lord was just what the queen mother was pointing to. In a certain way, she, too, prepared a path for the Word. People might say many things about Nebuchadnezzar, but at least he had been sensible enough to let the Word of God become a factor in political life. He had not banished that Word from statecraft, as Belshazzar had done by failing to keep the Lord's prophet at the court.

The queen mother was convinced that the Word of the Lord could shed some light on the affairs of state: "There is in your kingdom a man in whom is the spirit of the holy gods. In the days of your father light an understanding and wisdom, like the wisdom of the gods, were found in him, and King Nebuchadnezzar, your father, made him chief of the magicians, enchanters, Chaldeans, and astrologers" (5:11).

It is not to be denied that Nebuchadnezzar had impure selfish motives for elevating Daniel, and that the queen mother, who spoke of "the spirit of the holy gods," was clearly caught up in a heathen religious outlook. All the same, in one respect she knew exactly what had to be done: "Now let Daniel be called" (5:12). Not human wisdom or diplomacy but the Word of the Lord would cast light in the darkness and unravel the mystery. All human law and wisdom is destined to perish if it flies in the face of the Word.

And now Daniel appears on the scene. He begins with a history lesson that puts Belshazzar to shame. He points out that the sorry story of Nebuchadnezzar's humiliation should have taught Belshazzar something, especially since "you knew all of this" (5:22). It's the old story of Psalm 78 again. Daniel tells of the Lord's great deeds, of His strength, of the miracles He performed in order that coming generations would know enough to fix their hopes on God and not forget His deeds!

But Belshazzar simply laughed at all that history. Come now, Daniel, those are the old-fashioned ideas of our forefathers! We're living in an entirely different age!

Daniel also knew that it was not history but the Bible that would speak the decisive word. Therefore, he turned his attention to explaining what God's finger had written on the wall. He simply explained the message word for word, without adding or omitting a single letter. Daniel played the role of an honest exegete or interpreter of Scripture. He regarded any application of his own as unnecessary.

Although the words on the wall were short, they were powerful. They would give Belshazzar plenty to think about—if he would only listen! "The writing reads: *Mene, Mene, Tekel* and *Parsin*. The meaning of the words is this: *Mene:* God has *measured* your sovereignty and put an end to it; *Tekel:* you have been *weighed* in the balance and found wanting: *Parsin:*[4]

---

4. The reader may wonder where the word *Peres* in the revised standard version of this text comes from, for Daniel was supposed to explain the word *Parsin*. *Parsin* is the plural form of *Peres*. it was enough for Daniel to explain the singular form of the word. Literally, *Parsin* meant in two pieces. The kingdom of Belshazzar would be broken into two pieces; it would be divided into the two kingdoms of "the Medes and the Persians." It's also possible that the word Peres is a hidden allusion to the kingdom of the *Persians*.

your kingdom has been divided and given to the Medes and the *Persians*" (5:25-8 JB).

This explanation of the writing on the wall makes it clear that God had forgotten nothing, as the title of this chapter suggests. In the first place, God counted—carefully and patiently. The eternal God, who does not need numbers to keep track of things, was so gracious as to keep track of us by way of numbers. Although His dwelling place is on high, He was willing to come down to our level to such an extent that He concerned Himself with numbers. He made it known to king Belshazzar and to all the world—whether they were interested or not—that He does not arrive at His judgements lightly. His final decision is the result of a careful computation containing no errors. He counts just as carefully as a conscientious clerk writing up a bill. But once the balance sheet is finally drawn up, no new numbers can be introduced. The financial statement then becomes official, and the figure at the bottom is underlined. God is finished adding up these figures that reflect your spiritual condition. How does the financial statement look, Belshazzar? Are you in the red or in the black?

Let's listen to the next word—*Tekel!* You have been weighed in the balance and found wanting. God has indeed forgotten nothing and overlooked nothing. Not only did He count, He also weighed. Numbers are important, but they don't tell the whole story. Counting by itself is not enough; we must also weigh all the factors before we reach our final conclusion. In terms of numbers, the church has always been a minority in the world, but what results do we get when we weigh the church against the world? God does not want to be unfair, and therefore He makes it known here that He not only counts your years and your sinful deeds but also considers the question of *weight*.

God weighs the one consideration carefully against the other; He takes everything into account. The severity of the punishment depends on whether you have been exposed to the truth or not. It makes a difference whether your father admonished you and your mother prayed for you. That's why God weighs things. He examines the total content of our lives.

Would you like to know what's on the balance sheet, Belshazzar? After all the factors have been weighed with great precision on the perfect balance, the conclusion is that you are too light. Your life had no content; it was an empty life. Do you know what you forgot? You did not give glory to God who holds your breath and all your fortunes in His hands. Any life that does not have God as its chief content is an empty life—however beautiful it may look from the outside. It will be weighed in the balance and found wanting.

Parsin means *into pieces*. What can you do with a life that does not fulfill the purpose for which it was created? All you can do is break it into pieces. Any product that does not glorify its Maker but instead dishonours Him must be broken into pieces as quickly as possible. Cast him into the outer darkness!

When *our* lives are weighed in God's perfect balance, what will the result be? What have *we* devoted *our* time to? What is the content of *our* lives?

Take a single day of your life and try to assess its weight. What does it really weigh? Is it heavy with the fruits of conversion and the battle against sin? Is it full of prayer and self-denial and glorification of God? By all means, try picking up a day of your life. Don't just let it lie there. Don't be afraid to try! Go ahead! I'm sure it won't be too great a strain on your back.

Let's not try to dodge the issue by making excuses and pious declarations. We must learn to be truly frightened at the words on the wall, just as Belshazzar and his powerful lords were terrified. We are indeed afraid, aren't we? We certainly sing often enough about fearing God's holiness and justice. Do we mean it or not?

If we have reached the point where we do mean it, then we must raise our eyes to see what else God has written. Fortunately, He has written much more than those four ominous words on Belshazzar's wall. I know another set of four strange words in the Bible written by God's own hand. Those words are equally frightening. Yet, to all who believe they are glorious. The words are: "Eli, Eli, lama sabachthani?" The meaning of those words are: "My God, My God, why hast Thou forsaken Me?" Christ subjected Himself body and soul to the deepest humiliation and agony—the very anguish of hell. When

He was nailed to the cross, He cried out with a loud voice asking why God had forsaken Him. Because Christ was forsaken, God takes us to Himself and will never let us go.

For all those who believe, life has real content and substance. It is not found wanting when weighed in the balance, for Christ Himself is present in it. For me to live is Christ! In itself, my life is dry, dead, barren, and empty, but through Him it receives meaning and significance. Through faith it is as though I myself had achieved the perfect obedience that Christ achieved for me, for my communion with Him transforms my life. My life becomes fruitful; it is now dedicated to the service of the Lord. I no longer forget things as easily as I once did, for I know that God forgets nothing and will never forget me.

15

Applause or Amen?

Then Belshazzar commanded, and Daniel was clothed with purple, a chain of gold was put about his neck, and proclamation was made concerning him, that he should be the third ruler in the kingdom (5:29).

THE MOST WONDERFUL REWARD God's prophet can receive is not purple or gold or honors or praises of men but a response of belief and repentance. That's what they patiently await when they speak out. "To obey is better than sacrifice, and to hearken than the fat of rams" (I Sam 15:22). But Daniel waited in vain for this reward on his prophetic labors.

It's not as though Daniel wasn't rewarded at all. The heathen king Belshazzar was certainly generous to him: he dressed him in purple, and had a chain of gold hung around his neck. Daniel was even proclaimed third ruler in the kingdom. Belshazzar's father Nabonidus, who was leading the armies in war, was the first ruler, and Belshazzar himself was the second. Now Daniel was given the third place. No higher honor could be bestowed on him.

Daniel was promised this reward even before he uttered a single sentence in explanation of those mysterious words on the wall. In royal fashion the king kept his word, even though the explanation turned out to be a finger of condemnation pointed at him. He did not try to back out of the promise; in this regard he acted nobly.

Daniel had declined the gifts in advance, saying: "Your gifts you may keep for yourself; or else give your rewards to another" (5:17 NEB). In manifesting this prophetic spirit, Daniel demonstrated even more nobly than the king himself. But although he knew better, Daniel could not keep taking some pleasure in the honors offered him. In the final analysis, of course, this extravagant reward was a galling affront to Daniel—and even more so to Daniel's God. It consisted of *applause* for the talent and cleverness of the preacher instead of a sincere, penitent *amen* in response to the content of the message.

Let's take a careful look first at the reward and then at the man who offered it. As for the reward, it looks most impressive. The purple and gold signified that Daniel would be taken into the highest circles and given a lofty position, but the essence of the offer made by Belshazzar amounted to nothing. Had Daniel not testified that all the glory of gold and purple would come to an end, and that the kingdom itself was about to fall? That same night Belshazzar, king of the Chaldeans, was slain.

Daniel was to receive a position of great authority in a kingdom that was on its last legs and would only survive a few more hours. Poor Daniel! Even the glory of a butterfly with only a day to live would last longer than the honor bestowed on him. The frail and tender beauty of the lilies of the field does not disappear as quickly as the glory of his purple garments would. If Daniel had been enthralled by the prospect of the reward, if he had not lived in anticipation of a greater reward in heaven, he would have been the most deceived and pitiful person around.

Isn't it surprising how many people let themselves be mesmerized by that transitory glitter of purple and gold and titles, while never laying claim to any of the abiding treasures in heaven? In light of Daniel's short-lived reward, how foolish their attitude looks!

The reward promised and given to Daniel further illuminates the mind and attitudes of Belshazzar, making it completely clear that the ominous message contained in the "Mene, Tekel" did not get through to him. He simply didn't believe it. Hence Daniel was to be third in rank in a kingdom with no future. What Belshazzar was saying to Daniel, in effect, was this: "Daniel, you've handled my challenge very cleverly, but what you've just told us is nonsense."

It's not very likely that Belshazzar hoped to win the favor of Daniel's God at the last moment by bestowing these gifts on Daniel. It seems to me that Belshazzar's rejection of Daniel's prophecy is instead a manifestation of stubborn unbelief. The king stood before the prophet laughing incredulously, holding gifts in both hands. He was impressed, but he didn't understand that the time had come to extend empty hands to heaven in prayer. Poor Belshazzar!

It might surprise us that Belshazzar acted as he did. Daniel announced the judgment to him boldly, without batting an eye, but Belshazzar did not lock him up in prison. Instead, he gave him great power and authority. We would have expected an outburst of rage rather than this demonstration of friendliness.

There are two things we must be careful not to overlook. In the first place, Belshazzar was a *king*. Even if he was trembling inside, he would certainly not let it become apparent. Kings must know how to control themselves; they realize that they must remain calm and maintain their dignity.

All the same, I don't believe Belshazzar was actually angry at Daniel. To start with, he didn't believe Daniel's prophecy at all; if he had, he certainly would not have made him third ruler in the kingdom. Daniel's elevation was not intended as a mere gesture on Belshazzar's part: he really meant it.

Furthermore, Belshazzar's refusal to take the prophecy seriously paved the way for a genuine appreciation of Daniel. Belshazzar knew the Jews through and through. He knew that they dreamed of nothing but revenge for the destruction of Jerusalem, and they longed for the fall of Babylon. That was their first thought in the morning and their last thought at night. Now, Daniel was a typical Jew, for he knew immediately how to turn this mysterious inscription on the wall to his own advantage. Babylon was to be destroyed!

You have to admit it: he's quite a fellow! Isn't he exceptionally quick and clever? Hasn't he done a good job of exploiting that general confusion to Jerusalem's advantage? He's just my kind of man!

Belshazzar was sufficiently broad-minded to recognize Daniel's abilities. He appreciated the quickness of Daniel's fine mind, which was fueled by a dose of fiery Jewish nationalism. Belshazzar winked slyly at his powerful lords. Did you hear that? Did you ever see anything like it? They nodded in agreement. Everyone in that large chamber agreed with Belshazzar's praise of Daniel's sparkling ingenuity. Belshazzar, his lords, and his wives and concubines all joined in a standing ovation for this mental acrobat who displayed such talent as he "interpreted" the hieroglyphics on the wall and made a plea for his cause. Hurray!

All the people present stood there in speechless amazement at the *prophet*, but they paid no attention to his *prophecy*. The *preacher* became the focus of their adoration and approval, but they ignored the *message*, acting just as though it had never been delivered. They clapped their hands and stamped their feet in approval as they cheered for the man who had just become third in rank in the kingdom, but there was no amen drawn from the depths of their hearts in response to Daniel's shattering message.

Not one of them understood that Daniel had no interest whatsoever in becoming a ruler in *that* kingdom, that he only wanted to be a servant—a servant of the divine Word in the Kingdom of God. If there was to be any talk of "ruling," the burning desire in his soul was that the *Word* he had spoken should rule in the hearts of all those people. but that didn't happen.

A king of Nineveh had once been driven to repentance by the preaching of the prophet Jonah; those who heard Jonah preach wore sackcloth and put ashes on their heads. As a result, God's judgment was not carried out. But because Babylon's king came with costly gifts instead of the sacrifice of a contrite spirit and the spirit broken by the awareness of guilt, Belshazzar, king of the Chaldeans, was slain that same night.

The gestures of the king are still being copied today. There are lots of Belshazzars around. There are always afraid that they might eat and drink judgment to themselves by participating in a communion service, but they forget completely that listening to the preaching of the Word may lead to the same result. The Word is never without effect; it never lets us leave the church in the very same condition as when we entered. The Word either turns us to repentance or hardens us. It inevitably has the same effect if we close our hearts against its renewing influence and simply receive the content of the sermon for information—as Belshazzar did.

Look at the crowds of church people entering God's house. Why have they come? To meet God and listen in quiet reverence to what the messengers have to say *in Christ's name?* Do they say, "Speak, Lord, for Your servant is listening"?

Come now, it's the preacher who does the talking in church. We all know that most of the attention is focused not on the message presented but on the person who brings the message. He is glorified and condemned in turn for his preaching style. The people in the pew declare that one preacher puts a great deal of work in his explanation of the Scriptures, while another preaches superficial sermons. There is interesting preaching and dull preaching, beautiful preaching and not so beautiful preaching, covenantal preaching and evangelistic preaching. Sometimes we are irritated by the sermon, and sometimes we enjoy it. Sometimes we listen carefully, and sometimes we let our minds wander.

Just what did *the Lord* say to us this morning? To tell the truth, that's a question we rarely ask, a question we always manage to forget in our enthusiastic applause for the preacher or our vocal criticism of his style.

Jesus warned us to be very careful in our listening. James said a thing or two about being doers of the Word and not hearers only. He warned that it is dangerous to let the content of the sermon be without effect in your life. Daniel added that the most vocal approval and applause means nothing at all if it does not lead to the proper goal: "You have given no glory to God who holds your breath in His hands."

Preachers are given the reward whether they are deserved or not: each sermon gets a grade between "A" and "F." We have an extensive knowledge of each preacher's theological "tendencies," and we know just where he "stands." We are even brazen enough to pretend that a discussion of a preacher's theological inclinations is a spiritual conversation. But nothing happens and nothing changes: the one reward for which Christ's ambassador has a burning desire—repentance—is denied him.

Now then, is the figure of Belshazzar such an unusual phenomenon in our church life today, in which there is so much talk of approval and disapproval, in which each sermon is given a grade, in which there is a great deal of debate about who will be first, second and third in the Kingdom? It may well be that those talent scouts and theological inspectors wind up with no rank at all in the Kingdom, even though they are still children of God. Any simple believer who has no expertise in these things but listens with both shame and joy to the Word of the Lord will be greater than all of them.

Be very careful, then, in your listening. Not everyone who says, "Lord! Lord!" and admires the preacher will be permitted to enter the Kingdom of God. The ones who are allowed in will be the ones who *do* the will of the father in heaven.

"That very night Belshazzar the Chaldean king was slain." This warning is directed to all those who are vocal in their approval but do not raise the amen of the soul in a song of praise to God. The amen—not the applause—is still the criterion for admission to the Kingdom of God.

16

The Plot Against Prayer

*Then these men said, "We shall not find any ground
for complaint against this Daniel unless we find it
in connection with the law of his God" (6:5).*

WHAT DANIEL AND HIS FRIENDS had to endure at the hands of the authorities in Babylon was only one phase of the continuing struggle between the Christ and the Antichrist, the church and the world, light and darkness. A single glance at the "historical" section of this book immediately makes this clear.

In three of the six chapters of Daniel devoted to "history,"[5] we are shown how the Kingdom of Christ will put the

---

5. The first six chapters form the so-called historical section of the book of Daniel. The six chapters that follow it are notably

kingdom of darkness to shame. We see this in chapter 2, where we read about the stone that pulverized the colossal statue, in chapter 4, where we read about the humiliating illness of Nebuchadnezzar, and in chapter 5, where we read about the handwriting on the wall.

When we examine the events in the book of Daniel from this perspective, Babylon's repeated attempts to triumph over God are almost laughable. Babylon certainly does not give up without a good fight! The vain attempts made by Babylon—ultimately by satan—are described for us in chapters 1, 3, and 6. The well-known methods of cunning and force are also tried repeatedly.

Babylon's guile is already apparent in the first chapter. If Daniel and his friends can be turned into Babylonians in body and soul, then the church will be conformed to the world and Zion will be taken by surprise. When the trick fails, Babylon uses force: the blazing fire of the third chapter and the roaring lions of the sixth are examples of such an approach.

Yet the attempt to intimidate via the lions' den was not just a copy of the fiery furnace threat. There is a significant difference. The difference is not that flames were used in the first case to persecute the church while lions were used the

---

different and are often referred to as the "prophetic" section. These two parts of the book are to be distinguished but not separated, for the book of Daniel is also prophetic in its "historical" chapters!

second time. The real difference is that in this story to which we now turn our attention, a most unusual an extraordinary dangerous attack was made on the church. The church's enemies lunged at the jugular vein by trying to outlaw prayer. Since such attacks are still the most perilous of all, we need to investigate this matter very carefully. We, too, must be ready for an attack on prayer.

The Babylonian empire had gone under with Belshazzar, the Chaldean king, as we read at the end of Daniel 5. Just as Daniel had prophesied on the basis of Nebuchadnezzar's dream about the statue, a new Kingdom took its place—that of the Medes and the Persians. Darius the Mede was king now. The king is dead! Long live the king!

The Kingdom of the Medes and Persians was in essence just as anti-Christian as the Babylonians, the only difference being that it had a different name and a different king at its head. For the rest, things remained just the same, as we shall soon see.

Darius is the third king with whom we become acquainted in the book of Daniel. He is different from Belshazzar in that he is a figure to be taken much more seriously. Daniel describes him briefly as a capable organizer and an outstanding economist. He reports: "it pleased Darius to appoint a hundred and twenty satraps over his kingdom for the various parts of the kingdom" (6:1 JB). The empire would have to be redeemed from its earlier shameful condition; it would have to grow large and strong again.

The primary need of the kingdom was organization and an effective system of controls. The king did not trust even his best friends and highest officials. Plots and corruption threatening the careful reconstruction smoldered everywhere within this kingdom of iron. Consequently, Darius did not stop with the appointment of 120 satraps. These reliable public officials were in turn subordinated to three even more capable officials, who represented the kind of collective leadership, with Daniel as the dominant figure: "Over them [were placed] three chief ministers, to whom the satraps should send reports so that the king's interest might not suffer" (6:2 NEB).

Thus, we could perhaps regard Daniel as one of the leading members of Darius's cabinet. Darius had apparently learned a few things about him from different sources. He had heard how well Daniel had survived the king of Babylon. Darius quickly realized that he could make good use of this highly gifted man. The king even pondered the prospect of promoting him to a still higher position, turning him into what we might call a prime minister: "The king considered appointing him to rule the whole kingdom" (6:3 JB).

Of course, this aroused jealousy of the 120 satraps. Who was this Jew that he should be promoted before them? They also realized that their interests would suffer if Daniel were to be appointed prime minister.

We know from the parables of Jesus and from other sources as well that the highly placed officials of ancient times did not regard honesty as the best policy. When the governors of the various areas collected taxes from the provinces, a little money would sometimes stick to their fingers. The satraps had to report to the three chief ministers, we are told, "so that the king might suffer no loss" (6:2). Once Daniel assumed his position, the satraps realized that there could be no theft or graft if the money was to be turned in to him. He was not a man they could make a deal with, for he defended the king's right and interests scrupulously. With his aged eyes—he must have been 90 years old by then—he carefully reviewed all the financial statements submitted to him.

Before long the satraps tried to think of ways to get rid of this aged nuisance. "Then the chief ministers and the satraps began to look around for some pretext to attack Daniel's administration of the kingdom" (6:4 NEB). Slyly they pretended that their real concern was the welfare of the kingdom. They watched everything Daniel did to see whether they could perhaps detect some fault or mistake in his work.

Be careful, Daniel, for you're now living in a glass house! If you project yourself on being a "pious" person, just think how they'll laugh at you if they catch you in some misdeed or other. People are always suspicious of those who claim to be pious, for they're often the very people who commit all sorts of misdeeds under cover of darkness!

But what happened in Daniel's case? The beautiful thing about the story of Daniel is that it shows us what it means to put godliness into practice. We read: "They could find no ground for complaint or any fault, because he was faithful, and no error or fault was found in him" (6:4).

Daniel was by no means sinless. He was an ordinary mortal no different from you or me. He would have been affected very quickly by the corrupt environment in which he lived day by day if it were not for a secret source of strength that kept him from caving in: we read that "an excellent spirit was in him" (6:3). This excellent spirit was the Spirit of Christ.

The Spirit of Christ does not turn people into dreamers or idlers. The case of Daniel shows us that the contrary is true, for at age 90 he was still in fine health and held a very important position in a mighty empire. But the Spirit of Christ does not make a genius of anyone either. Instead, it turns people into believers who fulfill their calling on earth as faithful and willingly as the angels in heaven. It turns them into people solid as granite and valuable as gold because of how they live up to their calling.

How unfortunate that it is rarely evident from the lives of today's Christians that they possess an "excellent spirit." One Christian maintains that he works in an environment in which he cannot avoid evil altogether—regardless of all the preacher's fine words. A second has chosen the old saying "Business is business" as his motto in life, arguing that different standards prevail in the world of commerce than in the church! On the basis of such reasons, we surrender quietly to all sorts of heathen customs and practices. We take whatever we can get our hands on, in the same greedy way as those 120 satraps. Except for the fact that we attend church every Sunday, no one would ever guess that there is an "excellent spirit" within us.

Yes, that's what happens if you're a Christian in name but a Jew in your heart and bones. That's right, a Jew! The Jew asks about the letter of the law and is content once he has fulfilled his "Sabbath obligations," but the believer in whom an "excellent spirit" resides lets the Lord work in him through His Spirit so that he will be able to stay away from wickedness all the days of his life.

The reason that the world takes so little notice of the fact that there is a different spirit and therefore a different way of life within the church is that the plot against prayer has in large measure been successful. We no longer pray as Daniel prayed, saying at the beginning of our prayer, "Hallowed be Thy name," and meaning by it: "Help us to direct all our living—what we think, say, and do—so that your name will never be blasphemed because of us but always honored and praised" (Heidelberg Catechism, answer 122).

This leads us naturally to the second attempt to bring about Daniel's downfall. When the satraps could find no reason for complaint in how Daniel carried out his duties, they tried to use his piety against him. They said to each other: "We shall not find any ground for complaint against this Daniel and thus we find it in connection with the law of his God" (6:5).

A cunning trap was prepared. Daniel's enemies knew very well that he was just as faithful to his God as to his king. They knew he would be no more tolerant of compromise or chicanery in religion than in government. Hence, they persuaded the king to issue a decree *forbidding prayer.* They told the king: "We are all agreed, the presidents of the kingdom, the prefects, satraps, counselors and governors, that the king should issue a decree enforcing the following regulation: whoever within the next thirty days prays to anyone, god or man, other than to yourself, O king, is to be thrown into the lions' den" (6:7 JB). Thus, the proclamation forbidding prayer involved a most serious penalty.

The satraps were sure this plot would work. The king proved easy to persuade. Wasn't it flattering to him that for 30 days he would assume the status of a god in that he would be the one to whom all prayers were addressed? Furthermore, wouldn't this decree promote the unity of the empire? There were all sorts of nations within his mighty empire, and therefore there were all sorts of gods and religions. Wouldn't the growth and unity of the empire be advanced in a wonderful way if, for a period of 30 days, only one god was worshipped throughout the entire empire, a god whose visible representative was the king? There would then be one empire and one religion. All religious attention would be focused on the king. Wouldn't that appeal to your love of organization, Darius?

And what about Daniel? They know him well enough to be sure that he would never last 30 days without praying to his God. Actually, they didn't know Daniel as well as they thought. To say that he would not be able to hold out an entire month is an injustice to Daniel. In fact, he wouldn't last a single day, for every day he went on his knees three times to pray to God and confess his sins.

Thus, they had snared Daniel through his devotion to his God. The plot against prayer had been very well laid. The trap was set.

17

Prayer's Response

*Then these men said, "We shall not find any ground
for complaint against this Daniel unless we find it
in connection with the law of his God" (6:5).*

THE ONLY PURPOSE that the satraps and other officials had in mind when they hatched their clever plot was to get rid of a dangerous competitor. They knew that Daniel prayed regularly and would continue to pray no matter what happened. By convincing Darius to issue a decree forbidding prayer, with death as the penalty for disobedience, they figured they could get their rival into serious trouble. Thus, they would soon be rid of him.

Whether Daniel prayed three times per day, or ten times made no difference whatsoever to them. As soon as he was removed from his high office and was no longer able to stand in their way, he could meditate and pray as much as he wanted in his forgotten corner as far as they were concerned.

But we must not forget to examine the *background* of these events. The Bible was not written to tell us about the adventures of Daniel and the ingenuous plots hatched by people at Darius' court. What the scriptures intend to teach us is how things stand in the great war between the kingdom of this world and the Kingdom of God, between satan and Christ.

Satan goes about his work in his own sneaky way. The powerful people of this world are willing tools in his hands without even being aware of it. The devil's ideas are higher than their ways!

What the satraps saw as a *means* was to satan the *end* itself. Those earthly rulers reasoned as follows: "Let Daniel pray as much as he wants, as long as he loses his high position!" But the prince of darkness was thinking along different lines: "At all costs, Daniel must be prevented from praying. For the rest, it's all the same to me if he remains prime minister or even succeeds Darius as king." Satan is prepared to offer earthly kingship if that's what it takes to get people to stop praying to God in heaven.

We will soon see why satan puts stopping prayer at the top of his list of priorities. But at this point it's already clear that Daniel had to do battle with spiritual lions before he ever looked one of the king's lions in the eye. As a rule, we are more afraid of flesh-and-blood lions than of the invisible lion who goes around looking for people to devour. The ferocious roar we hear from the lions' den in the distance frightens us more than the ominous growl right behind us. We are much more afraid of the beast that can tear us limb from limb than the satanic monster who may well destroy our souls.

In many Bibles, chapter 6 of Daniel is given some such heading as "Daniel in the lions' den." This is indeed a proper title for the story—provided we remember that lions appear not only at the end of the chapter but also at the beginning. When Daniel still held his position of honor at the court and the king considered putting him in charge of all his ministers and governors, satan was lurking nearby as a roaring lion seeking to devour the prophet spiritually by forcing him to stop praying. Think of your position, man of God!

If Daniel had obeyed the king's decree, he would doubtless have been spared the lions' den, but he would have been devoured by a much fiercer lion. He would have been spiritually destroyed.

This shows us that the dangers we don't see are generally much greater than the dangers we do see. When we watch Daniel being lowered into the lions' den, we hold our breath in fear and anticipation. Yet, by that point the danger has already been overcome and the great fight has been fought. It is indeed a wonderful miracle that God preserves one of His children in the lions' den, but it is no less a miracle that God's gracious hand saved Daniel when all of Babylon—goaded on by satan—attempted to pry apart those two aged hands tightly clasped in prayer.

The great miracle of grace in Daniel 6 is that Daniel, the man of prayer, was able to go on praying. There need be no persecution of the church and no lions or devils with horns pursuing us for the church to be in great peril. The greatest dangers present themselves during times of apparent peace. In such periods we may well beg for the power of God's sustaining grace in order to keep from falling into the clutches of a roaring lion. We must always continue to pray, and we must see to it that the fear of the Lord means more to us than the favor of men.

The time has come to consider the question why satan was—and is—so determined to put an end to prayer. The prince of this world is not afraid of soldiers in full battle dress, but he trembles before powerless people on their knees in prayer. He knows that the strength of the children of God is to be sought in the very posture of weakness. He is well aware that the life and future of the church are dependent on prayer, for God will give His grace and Holy Spirit to those who truly seek Him without ceasing, who pray for His gifts and give thanks for them. That's why satan hates the sight of hands folded in prayer.

In Daniel's time, the ranks of those who pray had suffered a very serious defeat when Jerusalem was destroyed. Jerusalem was the site of the temple, the *place of prayer*, the place where

God was to be approached in His holiness. From Israel's earliest days, the smell of sacrifices on the altar had risen to the Lord of hosts, together with the prayers of all His saints. But once the temple was destroyed, this no longer happened. The fires on the altar of prayer were put out. There was nothing left but cinders and ashes. Thus, the Israelites lamented in exile that when God's enemies destroyed the temple, they roared like a lion celebrating a kill.

Was there no prayer at all going on anymore? Of course, there was! Daniel had taken a few coals from the altar at Jerusalem along to Babylon. In his room he had made a miniature holy place, where he kneeled in prayer three times each day. In this way he kept up his daily contact with the God of heaven and earth. The prayer of Jerusalem was continued in Babylon. A thread ran from Daniel's room to the One who makes His throne in heaven and establishes His dominion above the clouds.

As long as this thin thread was not broken, Israel still had a future, for God has mercy on those who call on His name. He cannot turn away those who knock on His door three times a day. How could God turn a deaf ear to His chosen ones as they cried out to Him night and day? If He did so, He would be unfaithful to His own promise, for He assures us: "Knock, and it will be opened to you."

Yes, as long as Daniel continued to pray, the lamp of the exiled Israelites would not go out, for the church lives by the grace of prayer. To that extent there was still room for a song of hope. The Israelites could remind themselves of dark days in Egypt from which God had saved them. The people who had been slaves found that their star was rising. But satan did not want such an exodus repeated.

At this critical moment in the history of the Kingdom of God, the great adversary tries to strike a decisive blow that will give him the victory. If only that single thread running from Daniel's room up to heaven could be cut! If only the one light still burning could be put out! Then there would be darkness everywhere. Israel would no longer have a future, and the Light of lights would not emerge from the world's dark clouds. Then Christ would not arise out of the nation of Israel. In Daniel's room with its windows open toward Jerusalem, the battle for the destiny of the world was being fought. If Daniel closed those windows, the door of heaven would be closed eternally.

What were the snarls and growls of starving lions in their den compared to this spiritual warfare in the prophet's own living quarters? Behind the seemingly simple decree forbidding prayer issued at the suggestion of the satraps loomed the abyss! Daniel and all who humbly fear God's name must keep their eyes wide open for the dangers on all sides!

If there's one thing of which we're not sufficiently aware, it's the power and importance of prayer. We don't make our prayers enough of a struggle. Praying three times a day means praying more than a thousand times a year. That gets to be a tiresome business, doesn't it? There are all sorts of quarrels at home and in the church standing in our way when it's time to pray—to say nothing of the sins we try to hide from the prying eyes of others, sins that cause us to avoid prayer or turn our prayers into curses. Then think of all the self-serving prayers we utter, the routine prayers, the prayers in which we show off. None of those prayers reach heaven; they burst like soap bubbles on the way up, which is why the devil lets us mumble such prayers as often as we like. Finally, let's not forget that even our best prayers are still impure, and that we need to ask forgiveness for our prayer life above all. Thus, we must speak of a crisis when it comes to prayer, a crisis that undermines the health of God's people. Prayer is the breath of the soul. When our breath is taken away, we die.

It's true that anyone who lives by prayer will not be affected by the plot against prayer. It will only cause him to go on praying even more fervently.

Do *we* fall into this category? Do *we* live out our faith? I'm very much afraid that if prayer were to be forbidden for a 30-day period beginning today, many of us would not regard this as a difficulty, for we attach more significance to a petition presented to a king or a high official than to prayer addressed to God.

It is frightening how many Christians live virtually without prayer. If you were to take a survey amongst young people or even the older generation—try starting with your own family—and ask people whether they begin each morning and end each evening with prayer, you would come up with some frightening results.

The failure to pray is the deepest cause of much of the misery in our midst. We no longer hear much about the joy of Christian living, nor do we read that the church is growing stronger year by year. The failures of the church and its individual members are a growing problem for the plot against prayer seems to be succeeding in our time.

Yet the condition of God's Kingdom is far from hopeless. We have more than a Daniel on our side—we have the One who sits at God's right hand and pleads our case for us. Of course, we should not jump to the conclusion that because Christ is doing so much for us, the prayer struggle is superfluous. The prayers of Christ, our Intercessor, do not disregard our prayers but take them fully into account.

Anyone who, by faith, participates in Christ's healing will also be anointed with the Spirit of prayer. Because of the great dangers threatening the church at present, such a believer will never stop begging God to pour out His Spirit of prayer on all flesh. Therefore, we should give a place of honor to those who pray fervently. They're usually not the ones who make themselves conspicuous in the church; in fact, you generally find them among the simple people of few words.

18

Perseverance in Prayer

When Daniel knew that the document had been signed, he went to his house where he had windows in his upper chamber open toward Jerusalem; and he got down on his knees three times a day and prayed and gave thanks before his God, as he had done previously (6:10).

HERE WE HAVE AN EXAMPLE of gallant disobedience. Once Daniel knew that the decree had been signed, he went directly to his house and prayed! His first reaction to this fearsome decree was to do just what is forbidden by man but commanded by God. He hurried to the forbidden place—the room in which he prayed. No matter how many unalterable laws of the Medes and Persians stood in his way, he would still give priority to the law of God, which we are never to break. Prayer comes first! One must obey God rather than man.

The Christian is commanded to pray. This is the commandment that we cannot get around; it's a mandate for everyone who believes. Yet, if you regard this command of God as nothing more than a vague appeal, if it represents nothing more than a good idea that you have never acted on, then you can start to compromise. You can argue that one must be open to a certain amount of give-and-take. Should there arise a conflict between God's commandment and human decrees, should your own interests suffer on account of your scrupulous adherence to the Lord's ordinances, should people laugh at you and refuse to take you seriously because of your obedience, then you might have to conclude that you can no longer let the law of God dictate what you do and refrain from doing.

But if those commandments of God set your heart on fire, if, through a wonderful paradox, they become a song on your lips and bring you great joy, that's an entirely different matter. Then your prayer life will never be interrupted by any decree forbidding prayer. Then prayer, for you, will no longer be a tedious formality we cling to, a garment we can take off for a while, a duty we can neglect from time to time. Instead, it will be a life-giving river that cannot be checked, a blazing fire that no amount of water can put out.

All the man-made laws in the world will not be able to put an end to prayer. The very idea of forbidding prayer is laughable. Who can command the lightning to stop? Who can order the thunder to be silent? Those who take this ridiculous prospect seriously are fools.

The decree of the Medes and Persians may include the death penalty for those who go on praying, but anyone who stops praying has signed his own death warrant for eternity. Prayer, after all, is the very breath of the soul. Only someone who has never prayed in a genuine way can stop at a given point in time. Life simply cannot be arrested in its tracks—but death need not be arrested, for it is already standing still.

Daniel would not stop praying even if there were as many hungry lions in the den as there are shingles on the roof. Just as it is impossible for someone implanted in Christ *not* to bring forth fruits of gratitude, it was impossible for Daniel *not* to go to his house and pray once the decree had been signed.

At first Daniel's course of action appeared senseless to us, but now we see that it is completely understandable. As soon as Daniel knew that the decree had been signed, he went to his house and prayed. If he had not done so, Daniel would not have been Daniel, the man in whom God had implanted an "excellent spirit."

Furthermore, Daniel knew exactly what he was doing when he retired to his room to pray: we read that he did so when he *knew* that the document had become law. He did not fall into a trap, and he did not intend to excuse himself by saying that he didn't know about the law. No, he knew about the decree and had already considered the consequences of disobedience. He knew that by going to his upper chamber he was putting his life on the line; he knew that he was walking to the gallows, so to speak. Nonetheless he proceeded to pray "as his custom had always been" (6:10 NEB).

It does not seem to have been a difficult, emotional decision for him. When a person is in a quandary, we like to speak of him as being torn by inner conflicts. If the Bible were a novel, these conflicts would no doubt be sketched out for us. Many preachers have speculated at length about the conflicts that may have raged in Daniel's soul. Yet the Bible says nothing about this matter. I am inclined to suspect that this is not because such inner conflicts are unimportant but because Daniel had no deep misgivings about his decision. It seems to me that Daniel would have opened his eyes wide in amazement if someone had asked him about the profound inner conflicts in his soul. "What conflicts? There was only one thing to do!"

What a man of God Daniel was! Weaklings like us who see problems everywhere are put to shame by Daniel. For him it was only natural to go on doing just what he had always done.

Such an attitude is both childlike and heroic. We see in Daniel the naive simplicity of the calm believer raising his eyes to God as well as the heroism of the man of faith who turns to God in prayer when he is surrounded by roaring lions and menacing snakes.

In Daniel we see the kind of triumphant attitude that will conquer the world. His is the victory of faith, a faith that does not become nervous or afraid, saying to itself that it would be better to pray in a less conspicuous place and manner in the future. (I could pray silently while I'm working—without even taking off my hat.) This kind of confident faith is also averse to showing off, and it makes no attempt to provoke or anger anyone. In this faith the believer acts normal— "as his custom had always been."

Daniel had an upper room in his home. Normally the windows of such a room would be covered by a grating, but Daniel had the grating removed so that his view in Jerusalem's direction would not be obstructed. Although he could not actually see Jerusalem, he could picture it in his mind's eye. Three times a day he prayed freely and boldly on his knees, confessing his sins to God "as his custom had always been."

Thus, Daniel persevered in prayer. Clever arguments to the effect that one can remain a believer even while abstaining from prayer for 30 days or that we should not take needless risks did not stop him. Although he was well aware that persevering in prayer might cost him his life, he went ahead with it anyway. The one thing that the decree forbidding prayer achieved is that his prayers became even more fervent and pressing. In this respect there may well have been a change.

It's enough to make you jealous: a great statesman kneels down three times a day like a small child before his God! If every government office contained one such person committed to prayer, the world would be safe from harm.

Although the content of Daniel's prayer in his upper room is not included in the Bible, we may assume that his prayer was in the first-place intercession. As you recall, the windows of his prayer chamber opened towards Jerusalem. Although his own life was in danger, Jerusalem's plight was the main thing on his mind. Jerusalem's restoration is what he pleaded for especially. Before God he confessed the sins of his people. Naturally he had confessed his own sins. A humble believer on his knees in prayer always begins with himself. Even the holiest among us—or better, *especially* the holiest among us—find reason enough to humble themselves in prayer before God three times a day.

Israel's communal sins had called down God's wrath from heaven upon the entire nation. Hence Jerusalem lay in ruins, and the people were in exile. If the Lord were to deal with the people according to their sins, the city and the temple would have no future whatsoever. But God had made promises about Jerusalem. Those covenant promises gave this praying believer the one thing he could hang on to—but it was enough. Luther said—and it almost sounds disrespectful—that he would throw God's promises right back at Him. But that's really what Daniel did too. Basing his plea on God's unchanging faithfulness, he begged for the restoration of Jerusalem and the return of Israel from exile.

Looking at this matter in such a light, we see that Daniel's prayer was truly the prayer of a believer. Jerusalem was a heap of ruins. If Daniel had actually been able to see the city from his upper chamber, there would have been nothing to look at but rubble, debris and smoking ruins—which is the exact opposite of what he was praying for.

It's characteristic of prayer that it expects the opposite of what the eyes see clearly, and the ears hear unmistakably. Faith sees the Invisible One—and therefore some unseen things as well, for no eye has seen and no ear has heard what God will do for those who wait on Him.

Daniel's prayer was also an obedient prayer. The Israelites were supposed to pray three times a day, and that's just what Daniel did. With the regularity of a clock, he knocked on heaven's door at fixed hours. What a blessing such faithfulness in prayer can bring is apparent from the parable of the importunate widow. This blessing has been experienced by all those who know what it is to pray without ceasing or doubting.

Many arguments have been advanced against such regularity in prayer. There is the danger of falling into a fixed routine, for example. Now, that's a strange thing to say! We're supposed to keep an eye open to the dangers of praying merely out of habit, but we remain entirely blind to the danger of the habit of not praying!

Sometimes we hear that prayer does not allow of regimentation. Prayer arises spontaneously in the soul like a sparkling stream high in the mountains. Therefore, don't prescribe a path for prayer to follow, for prayer creates its own path. Don't try to dig a special channel for the river of prayer, for prayer cannot be forced in any direction. I'm sure you've heard similar arguments.

Prayer cannot be forced any more than love. Yet the Lord *commands* the Christian husband to love his wife—and rightly so, for the spontaneity and openness that should characterize a husband's love is often missing. Selfishness so often threatens to clog the free-flowing stream of love with silt! Therefore, God has to *order* us to love one another. And He also orders us to pray.

Finally, Daniel's prayer was a humble prayer: we are told that he went down on his *knees*. The Bible includes this detail because it's also possible for someone to stand on his toes during prayer, to make sure that everyone will see him, as the Pharisees did in the temple. God has to have a great deal of patience with those who pray to Him. Therefore, mentioning the fact that Daniel prayed on his knees is far from superfluous.

Of course, it won't do us any good if we copy the *regularity* of Daniel's prayer without including the same kind of substance or content in our prayers. The question of the many lives that shed no light in this world, the question of all the darkness in the world, is answered here: open your windows facing Jerusalem!

19

Prayer's Victory

*He delivers and rescues, he works signs and wonders
in heaven and on earth, he who has saved Daniel
from the power of the lions (6:27).*

TO GET AN IMPRESSION of what prayer's victory really meant after the threat to prayer and Daniel's perseverance in prayer (of which we read in the sixth chapter of Daniel), we must consider briefly how the story came out. The happy ending is as dramatic as it is joyful.

The satraps who tried to trap Daniel succeeded. In fact, they managed to catch him in the act. The Bible condemns these elite men of the empire rather than Daniel when it informs us, not without a touch of irony: "These men came along *in a body* and found Daniel praying and pleading with God" (6:11 JB). What heroes!

Immediately they went to the king. Daniel, they informed him, was paying no attention to the king's commands. Like a rabid revolutionary, he was simply ignoring the king's edict. Now, that was the vilest way they could possibly have formulated their accusation. They didn't even believe the charge themselves—any more than the king did.

The king was not so much angry as disappointed when he heard their complaint. All day long he tried to think of ways to save his faithful servant, but there was nothing to be done. He was trapped by his own law that could not be amended or repealed, just as each sinner is caught in his own snares.

If we ask who has really lost his freedom in this situation, we would have to answer that it is Darius, the king. Not Daniel, the humble, praying believer, but Darius, the king trapped by his own laws, is the victim to be pitied. This proud sovereign was bound by the dark power of the laws of the Medes and Persians, which cannot be changed—no doubt for the glory of the empire! Daniel, by contrast, felt as free as a bird in the air even when he was being dragged to trial, for he knew he was under the protection of the law of his God, who has the power to close the mouths of hungry lions. Thus, Darius was actually in a worse predicament than Daniel, although Daniel was the one thrown into the lions' den.

We should think of this den as a deep, dug-out space surrounded by a wall. In the wall was an opening through which food was thrown to the animals. This opening was called the "mouth" of the den. It was closed by rolling a heavy stone in front of it. Since people who do not trust in God usually do not trust each other either, the stone was sealed. The seal was what made the execution official whenever someone was thrown into the lions' den.

Daniel won a victory through prayer. You might doubt this and ask why I speak of victory when we see apparent defeat. If Daniel does indeed emerge unscathed from the lions' den, *then* we'll be able to speak of victory. But why stop now in the middle of the story, when the resolution to the crisis in the drama has not yet come, when prayer's victory is not yet apparent?

Despite these objections, I maintain that prayer's victory is already present here. The triumph is greater at the moment when Daniel *enters* the lions' den than when he leaves it. To what extent Daniel's rescue from the mouths of lions is an extraordinary and additional answer to prayer is a question we can take up later.

The true victory of prayer can be summed up in one word—*tranquility*. What majestic peace we see in the figure of the prophet surrounded by wild animals! This strikes us especially when we compare his peace with the king's anxiety. Where is true majesty found—in the lions' den or in the palace? The question is answered quickly enough.

Look at the king returning to his home. He will not be able to get any rest. He will neither sleep nor eat, and he will be irritated if anyone proposes the usual pastimes. We read: "The king went back to his palace and spent the night fasting; no woman was brought to him, and sleep eluded him" (6:18 NEB). Very early in the morning, as soon as the new day began to dawn, he rose from the bed on which he had tossed and turned all night and hurried to the place where this sentence on Daniel had been carried out.

And what about the prophet? He spent a much more peaceful night among those ferocious lions than the king had spent on his bed. He was not tormented by images running through his mind, as was the king, who was frightened into wakefulness whenever he started getting drowsy. Instead, Daniel saw an angel. "My God sent an angel," he reported to the king (6:22). His voice was calm and properly respectful: "Long live the king!" Daniel had been sentenced to death on a charge of insurrection, and this one night should have been enough to actually turn him into a revolutionary. But that's not what happened to him. He prayed instead!

We see tranquility on one side and anxiety on the other. We see fear outside the lions' den and peace within it. That's the first great victory of prayer. Whoever puts his trust in God Almighty will remain completely calm in the midst of great dangers. He will declare boldly:

> God is our shelter, our strength,
> > ever ready to help in time of trouble,

so we shall not be afraid when the earth gives way,

> when the mountains tremble in the depths of the sea

(Ps. 46:1-2 JB).

The believer does not easily become nervous and anxious. When he does become fearful, it is usually because he is not clinging as he should to God in faith. On the other hand, someone who does not take God into account is always tormented by anxiety, even if he knows how to utter a few pious phrases on occasion—as Darius did to Daniel when he entered the lions' den: "May your God, whom you serve continually, deliver you!" (6:16).

How, exactly, was Daniel saved? It's hardly to be expected that Daniel would not pray for his own deliverance. No doubt he did pray for himself, and God heard his prayer. God sent His angel as an invincible guard, and therefore no harm could come to Daniel. When we read in the New Testament about heroic acts of faith and are told of prophets who "stopped the mouths of lions" (Heb. 11:33), we must take this as a reference to Daniel.

It's truly amazing what a believer can accomplish through prayer. Angels are called down from heaven, as in the case of Daniel in the lions' den. Think also of Peter in his cell, and the congregation in Jerusalem praying fervently for his release. Through the prayer of a believer, the mouths of lions can indeed be stopped. Never can a believer expect too much of prayer. The poverty in which many children of God live is a matter of their own free, sinful choice. It's nothing short of astounding what we can gain and accomplish through prayer if we will only try.

Yet this timely deliverance is not the highest triumph of Daniel's prayer; it is actually something extraordinary and additional or secondary. We would do well not to put too much emphasis on it, for if we do, the power of prayer may slip through our fingers.

We must not harbor the illusion that God *always* rescues His children in the hour of peril. The life of a believer does not always take such favorable turns as Daniel's life did here. Things often turn out much different for us than for Daniel: many are not extricated from the snare. The case of Daniel is most exceptional. No one should count on that sort of thing happening to him when his life is in danger, for he may well be disappointed.

God wanted this outcome in the case of Daniel. But it could have seemed much better to Him to let Daniel be devoured by lions. It's not a question of what suits us best but the question of what suits *the Lord*. The issue on which everything hinges is His glory. Had Daniel been able to glorify God more by dying the death of a martyr, then that's exactly what would have happened, just as many believers later died a martyr's death. But Daniel could be of more use to the Lord by remaining alive. Therefore, he was spared. And that's the *only* reason he was spared. God still needed Daniel a while longer.

The prophet was not yet finished making God's will known to Darius's world empire. That's why the miracle took place.

Whether the Lord will choose to deliver any of us in our hour of need depends entirely on the question what would advance the glory of His name the most. Let's be sure to keep this in mind at all times. Otherwise, we are bound to go astray in our expectations. Then it will seem that our prayers are not being heard, and we will start wondering why God chooses to save Daniel in the lions' den but not save us. In the end we will lose our faith in prayer as well as in God. We will be able to hold on to Him and to our faith only if we are fully aware that what happens to us is actually of little importance, and that the most important thing is the honor of God's name.

The fact that God's name was mentioned again in the official record of this world empire is an indication that God's honor was indeed furthered by Daniel's miraculous deliverance.

> Then king Darius wrote to all peoples, nations, and languages that dwell in all the earth: "Peace be multiplied to you. I will make a decree, that in all my royal dominion men tremble and fear before the God of Daniel,
> for he is the living God,
> > enduring forever.
> His Kingdom shall never be destroyed,
> > and his dominions shall be to the end.

He delivers and rescues,
> he worked signs and wonders,
in heaven and on earth,
> he who has saved Daniel
from the power of the lions"
(6:25-7).

The One who saved the church then and now and saved the world through His power is not Daniel but *Christ*. Yet Daniel reflected certain features of the Christ. He was accused of stirring up the people and was lowered into the earth. A stone with a seal was placed before his "grave." As soon as daylight began to dawn, someone hastened to his tomb and found that he had arisen from the dead, as it were. All of this foreshadows Christ. It's almost as though we were reading about the suffering and resurrection of Christ in one of the gospels.

If we, too, are saved in our hour of peril, it will only be because of Christ's descent into hell and resurrection from the dead. But the real proof that we have been saved is that our life, like Daniel's, reflects Christ, that we are conformed to the image of His Son!

20

Four Monsters in a Dream

And four great beasts came up out of the sea,
different from one another (7:3).

SPURGEON USED TO SAY that he read the newspaper to see how God was governing the world. That is indeed the best way to read the newspaper, for otherwise we would be too upset by what it tells us. If we follow Spurgeon's method, we can still sing as we read about all the disasters, war crimes and government blunders, for we know that God's hand is somehow guiding these human events.

The news reports that reach us every day confirm something that the Bible taught us long ago. It's not that the scriptures give us all sorts of detailed information about the course of history, but it is true that the major lines along which the history of the world empires will unfold are laid out in advance. The simplest child of God can give you a better account of where international relations are heading than the most expert statesman unfamiliar with God's Word. Because we enjoy the light of the Scriptures, we know what the ultimate outcome will be.

What we face is not endless progress but an inevitable decline. The struggle between the various world empires will eventually turn into a struggle between the kingdoms of this world, on the one hand, and the Kingdom of God, on the other. The current opposition between free, democratic countries and Communist countries will fade into the background when all earthly forces are turned against the Kingdom of God in total war. This antithesis is becoming steadily sharper as time goes on. The various governments are showing themselves to be anti-Christian powers. After a bitter struggle, they will finally succumb to the Lord and His Anointed.

This is the theme of the book of Daniel. The whole book is about the fading glory of the kingdom of this world as contrasted with the abiding glory of the Kingdom of God. This book gives us insight into the continuing struggle between these two kingdoms.

This struggle is the main theme of both the "historical" section of the book and "prophetic" section, which begins with chapter seven. The difference between the two parts of the book of Daniel is that the prophetic section looks at this matter from an angle of its own. The first six chapters deal with the struggle between the church and the world in historical terms, whereas the last six do so in prophetic and visionary terms. Thus, the range of ideas introduced in the latter chapters is greater. The Babylon of Daniel's day disappears from the prophetic stage, but the pagan spirit of Babylon lives on to the end of time in the successive world empires, which are usually symbolized by animals.

What Daniel is describing in Chapter 7 through 12 is not so much world history as redemptive history. The events that make up world history cannot be comprehended in terms of themselves but represent the scaffolding surrounding the church. This scaffolding is used in building up the House of the Lord, which will stand for eternity because it has been built according to God's plan.

Once we realize this, it should not surprise us that in Chapter 7 Daniel abandons the chronological sequence he had been following[6] and it goes back some years to "the first year of Belshazzar king of Babylon" (7:1). Belshazzar, as you recall, died at the end of chapter 5, and was succeeded by Darius. Early in his reign, Daniel, who had deciphered and interpreted the dreams of others, had a dream of his own, a dream

---

6. This is not to say that Daniel himself must have been the author of the book of Daniel. It is also possible—indeed, probable, given the fact that Daniel is so often referred to in the third person—that someone else wrote the book, making use of Daniel's memoirs.

that revealed both the course of history and the plans that his God and King had in store for the world. What was revealed to Daniel is of greatest importance. We are now given a lesson in history in the light of God's Word. Let's listen attentively.

After Daniel had this dream, he wrote down the "sum of the matter" (7:1) and left out the minor details. In the dream he saw a great sea that was being stirred up by the four winds of heaven. Thus, the sea was one large, foaming, swirling mass of water. Although the sea was already in constant motion even without interference, it became all the more turbulent when a storm whipped up the waves, especially since the wind came from all directions. In his dream Daniel saw a raging sea with huge, destructive waves rising and falling.

The reality represented by this sea is no less awesome and horrifying than the dream itself. We need only think of the millions of highly trained, heavily armed soldiers facing each other in the world's trouble spots, of airplanes plunging from the skies in flames, and of torpedoed ships to recognize that Daniel's dream reflects the world as it is. Here, as in the book of Revelation, the turbulent sea is the sea of the nations, a sea that foams and swirls but is never still. When the nations actually fly at each other's throats, it looks as though the ocean is raging so violently that storms are coming from all directions at once.

After the storm there is destruction evident everywhere. Many ships have gone to the bottom of the ocean. Dikes have been breached; and land is flooded, as the sea seeks more room and breaks out of its boundaries.

That's what happens when there is a storm on the sea of the nations. All the maps then have to be completely redrawn. Some countries disappear, while other kingdoms are expanded, and new ones are formed.

It should not surprise us that Daniel sees four great beasts emerging from the raging sea, each one different from the one before (7:3). They emerge not at the same time but one after the other, just as the various world empires succeed one another. Thus, there are major changes throughout the course of history. One great power fades away and is succeeded by another.

The four beasts arising from the sea are the various world empires that make their appearance through cataclysmic conflicts involving many nations. This is not a guess on my part, for later in the chapter we read: "These four great beasts are the four kings who shall rise out of the earth" (7:17). The idea that these beasts represent empires is really not so strange; don't we often speak of the Russian bear and the American eagle? When we use such phrases, we think mainly of the pride and strength of these creatures, but when the Bible uses animals to represent empires, it emphasizes the least attractive characteristics of these beasts of prey!

The four beasts Daniel saw were a lion (7:4), a bear (vs. 5), a leopard (vs. 6), and an animal so horrible in appearance that Daniel didn't know what to call it (vs. 7-8). Some commentators on Daniel have devoted great effort to figure out just what empires are represented by these four beasts rising out of the sea. Some of them have come to the conclusion that the four animals in Daniel's dream are to be identified with the world empires of Nebuchadnezzar's dream in Daniel 2, that is, the empires represented by the metals, gold, silver, copper, and iron, the metals of which the huge statue was composed. But once we note the fact that the fourth or last beast is not killed and does not disappear from the scene until the books are opened (7:10-11), that is, until the last judgment, we are more inclined to ask whether there is any empire *not* covered by Daniel's dream.

We would do well to look at these beasts in much the same way that we look at the sea from which they have arisen. This sea is not a particular body of water that could be located somewhere on a map; it represents the sea of all the nations. The beasts, likewise, are not particular world empires that must have existed at some time or other.[7] What the

---

7. In contrast to the vision of Nebuchadnezzar, where the king of Babylon is expressly identified as the golden head, the Scriptures here give us no indication of what empires might be meant. I do not mean to deny that one could begin by regarding the lion as a symbol of the Babylonian empire, the

prophet Daniel gives us here, in images drawn from the world of animals, is a striking characterization of the history of the kingdoms of this earth. He sketches all of human history right down to the last day, when the incorruptible Kingdom of God will put an end to all human kingdoms, when all earthly powers will be struck down by the "breath of His mouth."

This characterization of the world empires as beasts is striking and also makes us feel ashamed, both when we examine the vision as a whole and when we look at the particular features of the four beasts. When we consider the whole dream, first of all, an important difference between it and the dream of Nebuchadnezzar strikes us. A prophet of the Lord is an entirely different kind of person than a heathen king. The difference is even reflected in their dreams. Faith lives differently than unbelief and also dreams differently.

> bear as a symbol of the Kingdom of the Medes and Persians, and the leopard as a symbol of the Greek or Macedonian empire, for the resemblance between these beasts and the respective empires is indeed striking. My point is simply that the meaning of Daniel's vision is not exhausted by its application to these empires. It is also noteworthy that commentators disagree widely on what empire the fourth beast represents. Some think of the empire of the Syrians, and others of the Roman Empire. Because of what we read in Daniel 7:10-12, however, any identification of the fourth beast with the Roman Empire is out of the question.

The heathen Nebuchadnezzar had dreamed of succession of world empires. It was a beautiful dream indeed! In his imagination he saw the world powers as a majestic, gleaming statue. It was a dream of glory and greatness, of culture and beauty and power. He dreamed of gold and silver, copper and iron, steel and concrete.

Daniel dreamed too. He also saw the world empires in his mind's eye. But he saw them as beasts of prey rather than as valuable, glittering metals! He saw them not as embodying heights of culture but as possessed by the love of power and destruction. Daniel could never dream as beautiful a dream as Nebuchadnezzar. He dreamed instead of ferocious animals with sharp claws—a roaring lion, a hungry bear, a swift leopard, and a fourth, unknown animal even more ferocious than the other three!

This dream, of course, was not a mere fantasy on Daniel's part. It was a revelation sent by God; it was what God let Daniel see. Through Daniel, God shows us the world in the light of revelation unmasked and stripped of its external splendor.

The point of revelation is not just to inform us that the powerful rulers of our time and of long ago are by nature beasts of prey who lived by aggression and gobbled up smaller neighbors—despite their disguises and their pious declarations that they go to war only to ensure the creation of a more stable moral world order. All of that we could find out for ourselves without revelation, simply by keeping our eyes open. What God is telling us through this revelation is that the nations and the powerful rulers of this earth ultimately intend to direct their attack against the "saints of the Most High" (7:25), that is, against God's people and Christ's church. That is what the activities of these beasts finally lead to.

What this means is that the whole world is ultimately anti-Christian. One kingdom may lay aside its mask more quickly than another, but ultimately, it's only a matter of time. We will be hated by *all* nations, even by those that claimed to be fighting for religious freedom. That is what we Christians must realize. The Bible—and the account of Daniel's dream—was not written to tell us that the nations will destroy *each other* like wild beasts locked in mortal combat. Its message is rather that the wild beast whose rage is never calmed is stalking the turtle dove, the sacrificial lambs of God.

After these four beasts have made their impact on us, we are left wondering whether we can actually believe Daniel's description of them. We are told that the lion has eagles' wings, that the leopard has four heads, and that the unknown creature has large iron teeth. We quickly assure ourselves that such deformed monsters exist only in nightmares.

Let's not jump to any conclusions. Dreams are often deceptive, but Daniel's dream is not. True, we are living many centuries after Daniel, but we have already seen several monsters emerge from the sea of the nations, with its revolutions and world wars. Who would have foreseen the monsters of the godlessness and state-deification that have emerged in the twentieth century?

And what will the fourth, unknown beast turn out to be when the time of the third is over? Is this parade of beasts, the procession of monsters, a mere fairy tale intended to frighten us? The world may laugh at the prospect, and the church may doze off or indulge in nostalgia or spend all its energies quarrelling, but anyone who ignores the reality of Daniel's dream is like "the hungry man who dreams he eats, and wakes with an empty belly" (Is. 29:8 JB).

21

Unholy and Holy Aggression

The first was like a lion but had an eagle's wings. I watched until its wings were plucked off and it was lifted from the ground and made to stand on two feet like a man; it was also given the mind of a man. Then I saw another, a second beast, like a bear. It was half crouching and had three ribs in its mouth, between its teeth. The command was given: "Up, gorge yourself with flesh." After this as I gazed I saw another, a beast like a leopard with four bird's wings on its back; the creature had four heads, and it was invested with sovereign power. Next in my visions of the night I saw a fourth beast, dreadful and grisly, exceedingly strong, with great iron teeth and bronze claws. It crunched and devoured, and trampled underfoot all that was left. It differed from all the

> *beasts which preceded it in having ten horns. While
> I considered the horns I saw another horn, a little
> one, springing up among them, and three of the
> first horns were uprooted to make room for it. And
> in that horn were eyes like the eyes of a man, and a
> mouth that spoke proud words (7:4-8 NEB).*

THESE FOUR BEASTS REPRESENT successive world powers. It may be that they were meant first of all as symbols of certain empires appearing on the stage of world history during Daniel's time. Yet here again the sweep of the scriptural message is broad, for we are given a picture of the nature and destiny of the world's empires until the end of time. In fact, it's harder to specify which kingdoms are *not* meant than to indicate which *are*.

What we have here, then, is an overview of world history. In particular, light is shed on the opposition—indeed, the antithesis—between the Kingdom of God and the kingdom of this world. In the last chapter we limited ourselves to a global approach to these four beasts. Now the time has come to take a closer look at them one by one.

The first beast to emerge from the sea is the lion. Those who prefer to think in terms of a particular kingdom that this lion might represent have sometimes identified it with the mighty Babylonian empire of Nebuchadnezzar. Indeed, there are many similarities between that empire and the lion. In Nebuchadnezzar's dream, Babylon was the golden head—gold is the king of metals—while the lion in Daniel's dream is the king of beasts! This Babylonian lion also seemed to have the wings of an eagle, for it extended the wings of its power over all the known world: "King Nebuchadnezzar to all peoples, nations and languages, that dwell in all the earth."

"I watched until its wings were plucked off."[8] Thus the wings of this powerful creature are clipped, and it is no longer able to fly. In order to find such beasts robbed of their might, such powers cut down to size and even shattered, we need not turn to the chapter on Babylon in the history books. As we already saw, there is actually no world empire to which the dream of Daniel does not apply.

The image of the battered lion, then, is universal in its application. Again and again, empires rise, enjoy a period of glory, decline, and collapse. In our century we have seen a spectacular example of a lion with eagles' wings getting its wings clipped. The fate of this line is the destiny of all earthly kingdoms, however proudly such kingdoms may boast about their power and declare themselves invincible. We ought to remind ourselves frequently that the Almighty has decreed

---

8. The remarkable transformation of these beasts into human form, which includes receiving the mind of a man, as Daniel relates in his dream, is somewhat reminiscent of the illness of Nebuchadnezzar and his later recovery, of which we read in Daniel 4.

that the world and everything in it will pass away. Only the Kingdom of God is eternal and will not pass away:

> his dominion is an everlasting dominion,
>   which shall not pass away,
> and his Kingdom one
>   that shall not be destroyed (7:14).

Thus, one of the first and most important characteristics of the great powers of this earth is that they are transitory, that they inevitably lose their power and fade away. This is symbolized by the lion's loss of its wings.

Next comes the bear, which is a particularly ravenous and aggressive animal. While it is still busy devouring the prey it has just killed and still has three ribs between its teeth, it is already preparing for an attack on a new victim. This is what is meant by the words "it was half crouching"—as though preparing to leap. In its hunger for conquest and slaughter it is urged on by a "voice"—like the voice of a warmonger—that tells it: "Up, gorge yourself with flesh!"

Those who identify the lion with Babylon naturally equate the bear with the Kingdom of the Medes and the Persians. It's true, of course, that the Medes and the Persians were always interested in conquest and expansion. They were always hungry—hungry for land. But has there ever been a great power that wasn't hungry? Aggression is a characteristic common to all such powers. The one attacks and is attacked by another in response. All of them are on the attack, although they all complain about being attacked and threatened. If we were to take the words of the statesman seriously, we would have to conclude that they all love peace. Fortunately, the Bible here allows a mysterious voice to speak, a voice that proclaims the truth in a hard, merciless way, unmasking the powerholders in their craving for violence: "Up, gorge yourself with flesh!" They want to see blood! They want some cannon fodder!

The bear is followed by the leopard. Daniel saw that this leopard had four heads and also four birds' wings on its back. These two physical characteristics are an apt symbol of the third empire, which arose after that of the Medes and Persians—the Greek or Hellenistic empire established by the Macedonian king Alexander the Great.

Alexander was renowned for the surprising swiftness of his conquests. We could well apply the term *Blitzkrieg* to his military strategy. Hence, he could certainly be compared to a leopard making a lightning-quick pursuit and capture of its prey, or even a leopard that had sprouted wings to make it go still faster—no doubt the fastest creature on earth. If we go to recall that after the death of this world emperor, his kingdom was divided among four rulers, then the four heads of this beast of prey no longer seem so mysterious. They represent a kingdom governed by four heads of supreme authorities.

Here, too, the scriptures illuminate world history. This flying leopard with its four heads can also be regarded as symbolizing later powers, including, perhaps, some powers in our time.

Daniel gives an exceptionally clear picture of certain historical developments, namely, mankind's progress in the invention of new means of swift and radical self-destruction. This leopard is the third beast and represents an enormous step forward. The lumbering bear has given way to the swift, mobile leopard.

Today's armies move quickly in their motorized vehicles. Destruction is even more rapid when airplanes and unmanned missiles are used to bomb the enemy. In days, even hours, new territories can be conquered and occupied. Alexander the Great looks laughably slow by comparison.

Indeed, the flying leopard is an indispensable part of Daniel's dream sketching the development of earthly powers. Those four calculating heads are especially important, for what the one overlooks the other will be sure to remember. Together the four heads will invent a horrifying array of intercontinental missiles, rockets, and nuclear warheads.

The fourth animal, which is not identified by Daniel, shows us a modern world power in its fullest development. After the Third Reich comes a fourth, and the beast used to symbolize it seems unlimited in its capacities. It is grotesque and terrifying and extraordinarily strong.

I can well understand why Daniel did not know what to call it, for it resembled not only an animal but also a machine and even a human being. The animal features were indeed dominant, but the iron teeth and bronze claws (7:19) with which it crunched and devoured and trampled everything underfoot make us think more of a machine, whereas in one of the horns there were eyes like the eyes of a man. Furthermore, this beast had a mouth that "spoke proud words."

We are in a good position today to imagine such a beast, for we know what propaganda is. It's almost as though we see in Daniel 7 the frightening machines of war manned by people disguised as robots, machines that leave us wondering just what we are seeing. Nor are we unacquainted with the big mouth and the proud boast it utters.

It is said of this beast that it uprooted three of its horns to make room for a new horn coming up. Furthermore, we read that it was *different* from the other three beasts. The difference, as we shall see later, is that it directs its great power not just against other beasts but especially against "the saints" (7:21), the church of the Lord. All this development and technology culminates in total war between the Kingdom of God and the kingdom of this world. I will return to this fourth beast later to see "what the fourth beast meant," as Daniel put it (7:19 NEB).

Two important truths emerge from Daniel's dream about the four monsters. The first is that the world is lying to itself and to us when it speaks of the great civilization to come. In Daniel's dream, Humanism is dealt a devastating blow. There is indeed a development going on, but it is headed downward rather than upward. Daniel dreams not of angels of peace but the most horrible monsters. What arises from the turbulent sea of the nations is not an everlasting peace but a series of beasts of prey, each one more vicious than the one before. The culmination of human civilization is the unnamed fourth beast, which is at once man, machine an animal—the beast determined to destroy "the saints." That's the first truth taught by Daniel.

A second truth is that although this development brings out the antithesis between the church and the world in even greater measure, there is a remarkable similarity between the two. The similarity is this, that the Kingdom of God and the kingdom of this world both live by annexation. The Kingdom of heaven is always looking for more room. It respects no boundaries; it is expansionist by nature. As soon as the church loses interest in expansion, it has signed its own death certificate. Its quest for expansion makes it eager to embrace "all creatures," everyone. "King Jesus to all peoples, nations, and languages that dwell on the earth: peace be multiplied to you."

The church's growth is just as important a condition for its continued health as its preservation. Not only must the church guard its borders, it must go beyond them and take the offensive. By divine right, the entire world belongs to Jesus. We must reclaim the lost provinces of the Kingdom of heaven, which satan, the prince of this world, has wrenched from Christ's grasp. Therefore, aggression is the watchword of the church as well as the world. In this regard, the church is no less determined than any imperialistic power. In fact, the church goes even further: it refuses to declare that it will limit its territorial demands to any particular sphere of influence, demanding that all the world bow down to Jesus.

Yet, there is one great difference between the church and the world in this respect. The aggression of the church is holy rather than unholy. It does not depend on force. In fact, it renounces the use of the sword. It has no iron teeth or bronze claws. All it has is a mouth, from which issue not "proud words" or boast but the promises of the gospel, a joyful message for a weary world.

Finally, the church is assured of victory. The lion of Babylon is destroyed, but the Lion of the tribe of Judah will triumph in the end. His Kingdom is a kingdom of all ages. "The Lamb will defeat them, for he is the Lord of lords and King of kings, and his victory will be shared by his followers, called and chosen and faithful" (Rev 17:14 NEB).

22

The Throne in Heaven

I kept looking, and then thrones were set in place (7:9 NEB).

WHEN WE LOOK AT THE WORLD around us, all we see is Daniel's sea of the nations, over which the four winds of heaven have been unleashed. To our dismay, we see the nations making war on each other and devouring each other. This is what the dream of the four beasts of prey arising from the sea expresses in such a graphic way. That's what we see and hear. That's what we talk about, and that's what the newspapers are full of. Day and night there are reports on the radio and television about the frenzied activities of these beasts of prey. That's all we ever see—at least with the naked eye.

But the Bible also tells us about something not mentioned in the newspapers. The eye of faith trained by the scriptures is able to see more than this sorry spectacle. In his vision, Daniel also catches sight of a throne set above the sea and beasts of prey. From there all those monsters are controlled and kept in check. This is how Daniel describes it:

> Thrones were set in place and one ancient in years took his seat,
> his robe was white as snow and the hair of his head like cleanest wool.
> Flames of fire were his throne, its wheels a blazing fire;
> a flowing river of fire streamed out before him.
> Thousands upon thousands served him
> and myriads upon myriads attended his presence
> (7:9-10 NEB).

Most impressive! Above the turbulent sea there is a throne unmoved and unshaken. The throne is made of flames and is set on wheels of blazing fire. It is surrounded by thousands of angels. On this throne God Himself is seated.

Earlier Daniel was unable to name or properly describe the fourth beast because it was too horrible. He had a similar difficulty in describing the figure of God. The difficulty, of course, is not that God's appearance is so horrible but that it is so extraordinarily glorious and impressive. The prophet cannot find words to describe God. Therefore, he confines himself to saying that His robe was white as snow. He speaks of Him as one "ancient in years," for he is impressed especially by the majesty and dignity of the figure he sees. Presumably he speaks of God as ancient because such qualities are usually associated with age.

It is immediately apparent that this throne is a judge's seat, and that the one seated on the throne is the Judge of heaven and earth, who, as the highest ruler, humbles some and exalts others. But we also read that the actual judging is done by the "son of Man" to whom the "Ancient of Days" has entrusted the task (7:13-14). "The court sat in judgment, and the books were opened" (vs. 10).

The mention of this throne above the turbulent sea of the nations is not only intended to remind us that God will judge the earth righteously but also to convince us that what happens on earth is not a chaos of contingent events without order or pattern. All the threads of world history come together at this throne. God the Lord rules!

This is clear from various details in Daniel's vision. I have already pointed out that the turbulence of the sea of the nations was caused by the four winds of *heaven*. Thus, heaven is a factor in earthly affairs. Furthermore, we are told of those various beasts and kingdoms that "their lives were prolonged by a season and a time" (7:12). Therefore, they existed by the grace of God. Even more important, the length of their lives was in God's hands right down to the minute.

God's Word comes to Daniel and to us to calm us. The course of world history may appear to be a mess that can never be straightened out, but when we look beneath the surface, we discover that it is actually the unfolding of a single set program. Nothing that happens is more inevitable than what is commanded by the Lord. The commands that set history in motion come from the Lord's own mouth—not from some subordinate commander. Yes, the commands issue from the very throne that Daniel saw established above the raging sea of the nations.

There is a striking similarity between the prophecy of Daniel and that of John of Patmos. Before John sees and hears thunder, lightning, trumpets, bowls of wrath, cries of anguish, wars, uproar, and the greatest confusion, all combining in a deafening cacophony, he is allowed to see God: "I saw a throne standing in heaven, and the One who was sitting on the throne" (Rev. 4:2 JB). It is as though the Lord, in a protective, fatherly way, lays His hand on the head of His frightened child, who shrinks back in fear when he sees the raging sea and ferocious beasts. The child's attention is directed to heaven, and he is told: "There is a throne in heaven. The throne is not empty but is occupied by someone." We can be at peace, for God is King and He is in control. All things are in His hand. He is holding the reins.

But we must not make the mistake of supposing that we can *understand* God's way of ruling the world and figure out with our computers just what He has in mind for us. Both in the great world around us and in much smaller spheres of our own life, there is much that remains unexplained and mysterious.

Even if we have the assurance that we are the property of Christ, we should not assume that there will be no fierce storms breaking over our heads or wild beasts nipping at our heels. But we can be completely certain that nothing is able to separate us from the love of God. We can be separated from many things, including our most precious earthly possessions and our closest friends, but nothing can separate us from the Father's love. That love is the greatest of our possessions.

The throne above the sea of the nations tells us not only of God's control over world history but also of His final judgment of this world. "The court sat in judgment, and the books were opened" (7:10). Hegel declared that world history is the world tribunal, and in a certain sense he was right, for as the nations destroy each other, God is judging them. He humbles some and exalts others. But world history is not *the* world tribunal. There are too many scores left unsettled by world history. Injustice is still being rewarded, and the truth is still being crucified.

When we read world history as God writes it, we are inclined to put exclamation points and question marks here and there. We even want to cross some things out. But one day all the books will be opened. All the cards will be laid face up on the table, and a completely just judgment will be made, a judgment that takes all the circumstances into account. The sovereign Judge will weigh each factor very carefully against the others and determine who has already been sufficiently punished and who has not been punished enough. This world tribunal will also judge the four beasts. Kings, too, will appear before the judgment seat—but without their crowns. Dictators, presidents, and prime ministers will have to render account of all they have done.

Not only the great events of world history symbolized by the beasts will be judged but also your life and mine. The great things and the very smallest things, including all of our vain talk, will be scrutinized. No part of our lives will be overlooked.

God's books will be opened. Every human being is a writer, whether he knows it or not. Every day we make a new entry in the diary recording the events of our life. Each word and each thought is entered, without our even being aware of it. When the court sits in judgment, these books will all be opened.

We will all stand before the throne. Because we appear before a *throne*, most of the emphasis will fall on the question what attitude we have taken toward God's leading in our lives. Everything and everyone is controlled by God—the devils as well as the angels, the four beasts of prey as well as the "saints of the Most High."

But there is a great difference between these groups. Some submit to God's leading because they have no choice in the matter, because they dare not rebel. For them, the yoke is *not* easy, and the burden is *not* light. If they had their way, they would shake off God's leading immediately. Others submit to God's guidance because it's what they *want*. That's what eternal life means. Thus, it's not a matter of our will but of Christ in us. It is Christ who makes our hearts ready, willing and eager to live for God.

This glimpse of the throne in heaven gives us peace and assurance in troubled times. It also gives us true joy. Those who love God's law enjoy real peace and never beat their heads against a brick wall.

23

The Fourth Empire

The fourth beast signifies a fourth kingdom which shall appear upon the earth. It shall differ from other kingdoms and shall devour the whole earth, tread it down and crush it (7:23 NEB).

BY NOW IT WAS COMPLETELY clear to Daniel what the beasts emerging from the sea one after the other meant. The lion, the bear and the leopard represented successive world empires.

The turbulent sea of the nations breeds many monsters. Sometimes the surface is completely smooth and still, as the nations appear to coexist in peace and harmony. Yet, the passions of selfishness and hatred can flare up very quickly. Then the world turns into an arena in which savage beasts of prey fight it out to the death.

Like sensitive minds ready to explode, the monsters lurk beneath the surface of the water. At the appointed time they emerge to attack and devour each other. Even the best minesweepers in the navy's fleet cannot cleanse the sea of the nations of these destructive passions.

Humanism believes it can tame such passions. Its strategy is to deal separately with the monsters as they appear and thereby free the world from the threat they represent. But this is a vain hope, for once one monster is neutralized, three others will take its place, all stronger than the first. In the end the world will be even worse off than it was when the first monster was on the loose.

As long as *sin* is not overcome, the warfare will not cease and the beasts of prey will continue to make the sea unsafe, just as submarines lurking in the depths threaten cargo-laden ships in wartime. The statesmen who dream of a new world order, a sea without monsters and storms, a sea on which we can safely take a pleasure cruise, should read Daniel 7. This chapter will teach them that their hopes are idle dreams, for it shows us that things will get worse instead of better. The fourth beast, which represents the fourth empire (an empire that will not appear until the end of time, when human civilization and culture will have reached its culmination), will exceed all its predecessors in power and destructiveness.

Daniel was eager to know more about this fourth beast. Of course, he realized that, in general, the beast represents "great powers," but the fourth beast still left him somewhat puzzled: "Then I desired to know the truth concerning the fourth beast" (7:19).

The fourth monster was the creature for which Daniel had no name, the great unknown that looked so horrible and unreal that he could not decide whether it was a beast or person or a machine. It did have teeth, but they were made of iron, and it did have claws, but they were made of bronze. Furthermore, it had horns, but one of the horns had a mouth full of boasts and proud talk.

Daniel emphasized that the fourth beast was *different* from the other three. He makes this point four times (7:7, 19, 23, 24). We read: "It was different from all the beasts that were before it." It did not differ from the other beasts in degree only. It did, of course, differ from them in degree, for it devoured the *entire* earth, trampling under foot *everything* that stood in its way and smashing it to bits, as we read in our text for this chapter.

To use non metaphorical language, we could say that the fourth empire to be established on this earth will be a true universal empire that will make all other empires look pale and insignificant by comparison. This empire will conquer all other kingdoms and states, whether they be great or small, neutral or belligerent. It will be an empire without parallel in power and ruthlessness. As Prof. Hepp explains:

> Imperialism has become pan-imperialism; it is not satisfied with all it has. It demands *everything*—and gets it too. The national boundaries will be erased. Not only the small nations but also the large ones will be squeezed to death and dissolved in this all-inclusive empire. In our time democracy is still flourishing, but anyone who thinks it will survive to the end of time is mistaken. The dictator governing the world empire will not be a democrat but a dyed-in-the-wool aristocrat. He will not be sensitive to the will of the people, as the wisest rulers of our time are alleged to be, but will make his own will the law. He will show himself to be a despot. In comparison to him, all tyrants of earlier ages will seem easygoing. His commands will be broadcast to all parts of the world and obeyed everywhere. He will hold more power than anyone before him.[9]

Just as we sing that Christ will have dominion over land, sea, and the remotest parts of the earth, the world will be able to sing that this dictator rules all lands and nations.

Such is the difference in *degree* between this empire and the previous empires. But there is also a difference in *kind*. The fury of the fourth beast will not be directed toward the other nations only. Chapter 7 of Daniel makes it apparent that this beast will declare war on God and His church. "He shall hurl

---

9. V. Hepp, *De Antichrist* (Kampen, 1919), pp. 193-4.

defiance at the Most High and shall wear down the saints of the Most High" (7:25 NEB).

This war against the saints is ascribed to a single horn of the beast, a horn that arises after the others. Yet these horns do not symbolize later, separate kingdoms. In the light of Revelation 7, we must interpret these ten horns or ten kings as helpers or subordinate rulers who assist the dictator at the head of this empire.

Are you wondering what empire this fourth beast represents? Do you want to know "the truth concerning the fourth beast"? There is only one answer possible: it represents the kingdom of the *Antichrist*. This is clear from what Daniel tells us about the beast.

In the first place, this empire is the *last* one to appear on the earth. After the fourth beast, Daniel sees no more monsters emerging from the sea. There is nothing more to await from below. There is, of course, still something to await from above, for the Son of man will come on the clouds of heaven (7:13) to put an end to this fourth empire once and for all (vs. 26). That's also what the New Testament teaches. Paul writes that Christ will not return until the "man of sin," the "son of perdition" is revealed (II Thess. 2:3-4). Paul is referring here to the Antichrist, a man of flesh and blood, a tyrant and world dictator lording over the whole earth and the church and conducting himself like the revolting monster in Daniel's vision.

In the second place, it is said of this beast that it "shall think to change the times and the law" (7:25). What is meant by changing the "times" is that the Antichrist will try to take the control of world events into his own hands completely, usurping the role of providence, as it were. Paul tells us that the Antichrist proclaims himself God and seeks to take God's place.

As for changing the law, it refers to his effort to transform human life totally. The Christian foundations must be destroyed. What was once condemned as wrong will be praised as right. What was once regarded as shameful will then be seen as honorable. What was once shunned as a lie will then be hailed as the truth. Everything will be turned upside down. Therefore, the Antichrist is also spoken of as the "man of lawlessness," the "lawless one" (II Thess. 2:3,8).

Although the anti-religious purpose of the Antichrist is already fully apparent, it becomes even clearer when we consider his struggle against the "saints of the Most High." He sinks his teeth into the church. We read that he will "wear out" the saints of the Most High (7:25). The prophet used a memorable phrase here: the saints will be exhausted, used up. The Antichrist will fight a "cold war" against the church, a war of attrition. He will rely on subtle and refined forms of oppression designed to break the most stubborn resistance. Even the chosen ones would finally buckle if the time were not shortened.

This chapter of Daniel agrees fully with what the Bible says elsewhere about the Antichrist. Christ Himself declared: "It will be a time of great distress; there has never been such a time from the beginning of the world until now, and will never be again" (Matt. 24:21 NEB). Prof. Hepp writes:

> Nero's night festivals, at which Christians wrapped in flammable materials served as torches, and the stakes which those who confessed the truth were burned in latter ages will seem mild treatment when compared to the martyrdom to come. A new book of the martyrs will have to be written, one that goes far beyond its predecessor in describing horrible things. The church will again learn what it means to bear a cross.[10]

Daniel also tells us how long the Antichrist will rule. This fourth kingdom will retain its power for "a time, two times, and a half time" (7:25).

Now, we must resist the impulse to start figuring out just what this means in numerical terms, as some of the church fathers did, who then concluded that the tyranny of the Antichrist would last exactly 3 1/2 years. The Bible is using figurative language here. When Daniel speaks of the oppression which the church will have to suffer, he means that at first it will seem a very long time: the oppression will last for "a time." When the church then begs God in prayer for relief, it will suf-

---

10. *De Antichrist*, p. 211.

fer Israel's fate in Egypt: the oppression will be doubled, that is, it will last twice as long again. That's what Daniel means by "two times." But even then, the end will not come. A third period will begin, in which the oven will be made still hotter. By then the issue will be one of life or death. The church will be on the brink of complete collapse and eradication.

Suddenly Christ will intervene in power. The third period will be interrupted dramatically. This is the "half a time" of which Daniel speaks, the time which Jesus said would be "cut short." But to the believers of those last days, it will seem as though there is no end in sight.

We are told about the duration of the oppression in terms of "times" that cannot be translated into periods of a certain length. But we are assured that the end will indeed come. The turtle dove will not be surrendered to the wild beasts. In the midst of the lions, bears, leopards, and unidentifiable monsters, the Good Shepherd goes about His work, laying down His life for the sheep and seeing to it that not one of them is taken away from Him.

When Jesus returns, it will be the end for the Antichrist. "Then the court shall sit, and he shall be deprived of his sovereignty, so that in the end it may be destroyed and abolished" (7:26 NEB).

24

The Things to Come —the World

But he said to me, "understand, O son of man, that the vision is for the time of the end" (8:17).

THE DREAM IN CHAPTER 7 of Daniel calls attention to the Antichrist, who is to appear at the end of time, while the vision in chapter 8 shows us what the world and the church will look like then. Thus, Daniel 8 gives us a scriptural look at the things to come.

In the third year of Belshazzar, three years after the remarkable dream of the four beasts, the prophet received the vision of the ram and the he-goat. At that time, he was in the city of Susa, which is on the Ulai, a river that is probably a channel linking the two rivers flowing around the city.

In this vision Daniel is shown what will happen when "the time of the end" arrives, a time that is to come after "the end of the wrath" (8:19 NEB). What is meant by the "wrath" is probably something akin to the divine wrath felt by the Israelites when they were sent into exile in Babylon. In other words, Daniel is being warned that at the end of the 70-year period, there will not be peace and amity immediately. The messianic period will not begin right away, for many horrible things must happen first. Through the vision, Daniel was being prepared for those events.

This revelation about the future is just as important for us as for Daniel! The lines laid down here can be projected to the *end of time*. What Daniel saw prophetically was *provisionally* fulfilled after the period of the exile but will not be fulfilled *fully* until the end of time and the day of the Son of man.

From the mouth of the angel Gabriel, who appears here as the interpreter of the vision (8:16), we learn that near the end there will be a king who will cause "fearful destruction" (vs. 24). This king is no one other than the fourth beast of Daniel 7, whom we recognize as the Antichrist.

We are now told two more things about the time of his reign. First, he will appear when "sin is at its height" (8:23 NEB), that is, when the degeneration of the human race has reached its climax. This tells us something about the life of the "church" at that time. Furthermore, he will come to power at "the latter end of their rule," that is, after the times of the kingdoms represented symbolically in the vision by the ram and the he-goat. This tells us something about the life and of the rest of the world at that time. As soon as the church and the world have reached this point, it will be time for the Antichrist to make his appearance.

We will look first at the life of the world. What does this struggle between the ram in the he-goat mean?

Daniel saw a ram with two powerful horns, one bigger than the other. The ram charged northward, westward, and southward (8:3-4).

This animal represents people—and also kings, as we shall see later. It is clear from the outset that it symbolizes a world power charging out of the east to attack the rest of the world on three fronts, butting others out of the way with its horns. It makes forays to the north, west and south. The ram "did as he pleased and magnified himself" (8:4). That's what Daniel saw—willfulness, land grabbing, and military might. There stood the powerful ram—proud and unassailable. "No animal could stand up to it, nothing could escape it" (vs. 4 JB).

But things change quickly in human history. Hardly has the ram appeared on the stage of world history than a he-goat approaches from the west (8:5). This western world power charges the power from the east with such speed that its feet hardly seem to touch the ground and with such *force* that the powerful ram is trampled underfoot. "The he-goat flung it to the ground and trampled on it, and there was no one to save the ram" (vs. 7 NEB). This is the same language that was applied to the ram's victories a moment before.

That's the irony of history. That's just how things go with the power of the strong. When God moves the pieces on the chess board around, what difference do all the horns and bombers and battleships make? Even the most courageous horse may fall in battle, however quick and agile it is. By itself no horse or weapon can win the battle. No earthly strength is enough to carry the day.

Thus, the powerful ram is defeated by the even more powerful he-goat. The one seated in the heavens laughs at the sight of all those horns and weapons, all those submarines and jet fighters. God the Lord rules!

Again, we see the story of the rise and fall played out before our eyes. "Then the he-goat magnified himself exceedingly; but when he was strong, the great horn was broken, and instead of it there came up four conspicuous horns toward the four winds of heaven" (8:8). Thus, the western world power symbolized by the he-goat fell from the heights too. We are not told how this fall took place, but his strength was broken suddenly. The great horn was shattered and made way for four others, "but not with power comparable to his" (vs. 22 NEB). In other words, the great kingdom was fragmented and transformed into four smaller kingdoms.

That's how Daniel sees the course of world history. He sees horns, horns, and more horns! There are horns to be seen on all sides! The East clashes with the West, and the West attacks the East. We see a frantic arms race. One kingdom magnifies itself, and the other responds with a display of belligerence and power.

From Daniel's vision we might well get the impression that nations have nothing but horns and produce nothing but weapons to attack each other. In those tense situations where horn confronts horn, conflicts are inevitable. Battle after battle rages, with both sides suffering defeat and celebrating victories. Nation succeeds nation as the greatest world power. First the ram is the mightiest power in all the world, and then the he-goat, who is in turn overthrown by another upheaval.

But this is not the most important thing about Daniel's vision. What made the greatest impression on Daniel was not the strength of the horns but their *fragility*. The horns were *broken* one after the other, to symbolize how kingdom after kingdom is destroyed. The dominant impression created by the vision is not one of victory but one of defeat! Each victor is vanquished in turn, as Daniel watches the nations destroying each other. When the smoke and the warfare clear away, there is no horn that has not been broken and no power that does not lie dying.

By destroying each other, the eastern and western powers prepare the way for the last king, the king who will rule the entire world, the king who will appear "at the latter end of their rule" when "sin is at its height." the king is the Antichrist!

The powerlessness and exhaustion of the nations that wasted their strength in wars against each other is used cleverly by the "king of bold countenance" whom Daniel sees at the end of his vision (8:23). He establishes his dictatorship on the ruins of the weakened nations.

In this vision, the "king of bold countenance" is represented by a small horn that sprouts from the four mighty horns arising from the he-goat. The anti-Christian state will not come down from the sky! Yet there will be an important difference between this kingdom and all previous kingdoms. Whereas all the earlier kingdoms fought and destroyed each other, this king will concentrate his attack on the "glorious land" (8:9), that is, the holy land and the people of God. Not satisfied with this, he will even seek to manifest his power in a struggle with heaven (vs. 10). He is free to do so because his hands are not occupied with the earth, where he is the sole, unchallenged ruler. The identity of this last king is quite clear by now.

Gabriel, the interpreter, gives us the key to the vision. "The two-horned ram which you saw signifies the kings of Media and Persia" (8:20 NEB). Now, the Kingdom of the

Medes and Persians was indeed established after Belshazzer's death. It went on to become master of three fourths of the known world, pushing ahead with its horns like the powerful ram.

"And the he-goat is the king of Greece" (8:21). With incredible speed—just like the goat in the vision, which hardly appeared to be touching the ground—Alexander the Great, king of Greece, then proceeded to conquer the world.

Gabriel went on to explain: "As for the horn that was broken, in place of which four others arose, four kingdoms shall arise from his nation, but not with his power" (8:22). That prophecy was also fulfilled. Just as Gabriel said, the Greek or Macedonian empire was split up into four parts, each part having its own ruler.

The confusion of this era was exploited by Antiochus Epiphanes to consolidate and expand his own power. He is the small horn that grew exceedingly great, encroaching on the "glorious land" as the tormentor and persecutor of the Jews and setting himself up in opposition to the Ruler of rulers.

We must not underestimate the depth of the Scriptures—by supposing that this is nothing more than a prophecy about the history of the Jewish people in the centuries immediately after Daniel's time. These visions would not have been preserved for us if the events described in them were not a foreshadowing of what the church will face at the end of time.

We, too, will have to face this fearsome king. Antiochus Epiphanes is a prefiguration and forerunner of the arch enemy of the church, the dictator of the entire world who will rule during the waning hours of world history. That dictator's name is Antichrist.

From this vision we get an indication of when to expect him. Like Christ, the Antichrist is waiting for the "fullness of time." His time will come when the conditions in the world have degenerated to the point sketched for us in the vision. He is waiting for a world in which the horn looms large, a world in which the ram and the he-goat and various other creatures are locked in mortal combat—combat involving harsh realities rather than mere phenomenon in a vision. In the time leading up to the Antichrist, such powers and struggles will not just be fragments of ancient history but the first item in the radio and television news broadcasts. Every man will do as he pleases, showing off his own power and then going down to defeat, so that all the nations ultimately bury each other in a mass grave.

When all of this has come to pass, it will be time for the Antichrist. He's watching developments very carefully and waiting for the right time, the moment when the nations will have beaten each other almost to death.

When we read about the ram, the he-goat, and the waiting, leering "third" power, we are inclined to fill in the names. We should resist this impulse. What we must do instead is keep each other alert so that we will be able to read the signs of the times. Jesus told us what those signs are—wars and rumors of wars. And that's not the worst of it: the worst is what comes afterward.

On the deserted battlefields where the nations have found a common grave, the figure of the Antichrist appears. We regard those wars as horrible in themselves, but they are only the beginning of the suffering to come. We would do well to face the cold facts with both eyes open. The truth shall make us free. But are we ready for the truth? Are we ready for the enemy who will attack not our country but the church of the Lord? That's the great war still to come.

25

The Things to Come —the Church

When the transgressors have reached their full measure... (8:23).

IN VISIONARY LANGUAGE, the eighth chapter of Daniel shows us what things will look like in the world and the church just before the return of Christ. In those days the anti-Christian state will reign supreme on earth, a state embracing all the peoples and nations. The head of this state will be the Antichrist himself.

This Antichrist, the man of sin who was foreshadowed by Antiochus Epiphanes, the arch enemy of the Jews, will found his world empire on the ruins of the great powers that have destroyed each other by fire and the sword. The battlefield of the nations, drenched with the blood of the soldiers, is the only suitable foundation for the throne of this world dictator.

But what will the church look like when that time comes? Daniel characterizes the time of the Antichrist as a period in which "the transgressors have reached their full measure," by which he means that sin's degeneration will have reached its low point. Like the nations that have bled to death, the church cannot hold out against the Antichrist. Nothing pleases the great enemy of God's people more than the growth and apostasy and unbelief within the church.

The great falling away among the people of the Lord depicted in Daniel 8 applies first of all to the spiritual condition of the Jewish people during the time of Antiochus Epiphanes. Just as the service of Baal promoted by Ahab and Jezebel threatened to squeeze the religion of the patriarchs to death, the long arms of Greek culture reached out to gather up the children of the covenant in their embrace. Many Jews were greatly impressed by Greek culture. Adopting the customs and ethos of the heathen Greeks was the thing to do in refined society.

But because oil and water do not mix, because no accommodation is possible between Christ and Belial, the inevitable consequence of such an attitude toward Greek culture was that the worship of God was forced into a corner. Where true religion survived at all, it was reduced to nothing more than a preservation of certain forms and customs. Eventually, the religion of externals achieved its fullest development in Phariseeism.

A people whose soul had already been cut down, so to speak, were not in a position to offer much resistance to Antiochus Epiphanes, that destroyer of the church. This despot, who was a fiery proponent of Greek culture and an avowed enemy of religion, used all the means at his disposal in his effort to wipe out the Jewish religion.

One of the psalmist's complaints is that both force and cunning are used against God's people. Muscle and guile are always the tried-and-true weapons used against the church of the Lord. If cunning does not work, force is applied. When force fails, the church's enemies turned to cunning.

Daniel tells us that Antiochus was "harsh and grim, a master of stratagem" (8:23 NEB). That he was harsh and grim means that he was not afraid to employ violent methods. That he was a "master of stratagem" or that he "understood riddles," as we read in another translation, means that he was a gifted diplomat and an expert in intrigue, a man who knew how to use trickery and deceit to reach his goal.

Antiochus started with cleverness and cunning, for he knew that this is the best method of infiltrating the church and secularizing it. As soon as the church has become like the world, its *raison d'être* is gone. Therefore, Antiochus not only propagated Greek culture with all his might but also made a point of giving the choices to government positions to Jews sympathetic to Greek culture. Naturally this method was a great success, for when the question of a livelihood enters the picture, "principles" often become inoperative. It shouldn't surprise us either that Daniel prophesies, "He shall succeed in what he does, and destroy mighty men and people of the saints" (8:24).

Half the Jews gave Antiochus no trouble at all: they capitulated as soon as a finger was pointed in their direction. But as in every age, there was a core of faithful believers. They were only a small group, this "remnant chosen in God's grace," but they had enough courage to strenuously oppose the attempts to destroy the church.

Then Antiochus changed his tactics. The friendly smile disappeared from his face as the gentle persuader became "harsh and grim." Now he would use force to bring those stubborn fanatics to their knees. Thus, a period of fierce religious persecution began, as cunning was replaced by strong arm tactics.

A decree was issued that all holy books of the Old Testament were to be burned. Thus, Daniel's words were literally fulfilled, for he had prophesied that the truth would be cast down to the ground (8:12). Religious ceremonies like prayer and circumcision were declared punishable offences. The penalties were severe: sometimes a mother who dared to have her child circumcised would be brought to the place of judgment with the corpse of her baby tied around her neck.

The most effective step taken by Antiochus was the suppression of the regular offering (8:11), the perpetual sacrifice, the burning sacrifice that had to be lit every morning and every evening, according to the law. To let this practice, go would mean a complete break with true religion. Public worship services would then be impossible.

Daniel tells us: "The host was given over to it together with the continual burnt offering through transgression" (8:12). This is certainly puzzling language. It appears that what Daniel meant is this: not only was the service of the Lord forbidden, an apostate form of worship was established in its place, an adoration of satan in place of the worship of the living God—something that was carried out in the temple at that! It was this temple of the Lord of which the Savior also said, "Let the reader understand" (Matt. 24:15).

From Antiochus to the Antichrist is but a single step. Earlier I warned against underestimating the depth of the Scriptures and assuming that what we have here is nothing more than a chapter in the history of the Jewish nation. These versions would not have been preserved for us in Scripture if the events in them were not a foreshadowing of what will happen to us at the end of time. We, too, will have to face this king. Antiochus Epiphanes is only a type or a forerunner of the archenemy of the church who will rule on earth when the sunset of world history comes. He is a prefiguration of the ruler whose name is Antichrist.

Like the Christ, the Antichrist is waiting for the "fullness of time." His time will come when the condition of the church is what this chapter describes for us. Just as Greek customs and ethos pushed aside the religion of the patriarchs during the time of Antiochus, the secularization of the church will have progress very far indeed by the time the Antichrist appears. Only in a time of fearful decay could the "man of sin" enjoy such success in his effort to make the church worldly. Just as a general can make little use of his military expertise in a time of peace, so the Antichrist could not achieve much against the church in a time of strong and vibrant faith. When the church begins to decline spiritually, however, the Antichrist will breathe the stinking air on which he thrives. He will then be able to enter Zion's gates without a struggle, for the traders inside the fortress will be eager to surrender.

Jesus sketched this spiritual state of affairs by saying: "they ate, they drank, they married, they were given in marriage... They planted, they built" (Luke 17:27-8). Are we then to condemn those activities as sin? Of course not! Eating, drinking, marrying, and working are all indispensable parts of life. The sinful thing about these people of whom Jesus speaks is that there is nothing more to it for them. Their horizon goes no further. They no longer take heaven into account or regard themselves as citizens of heaven. Instead, they concern themselves exclusively with the earth. The ideal of "seeking the things that are above" is given up as old-fashioned, pietistic, irrelevant.

We need not look for spectacular sins as evidence of the secularization of the church, for in the church you find nice people who will have nothing to do with debauchery. You certainly can't accuse them on that score. What you *can* accuse them of, however, is the insidious sin of conforming more and more to the world. Not the law of the Lord but the world's way of thinking becomes normative for life. Everyone looks out for himself, and no one puts the welfare of others ahead of his own. What is this individualism but conforming to the world? Egoism flourishes, and the Savior's prophecy that the love of many will grow cold is borne out. Even if the ecclesiastical forms are preserved intact, the insides have become so rotten that the Antichrist will succeed in his very first attack.

But the forms will not remain intact to the end. Daniel's prophecy that the "continual burnt offering" will be taken away when this world's late evening comes will be fulfilled completely. In our country we are still allowed to hold our worship services and give thanks to God without interference—even though we often do so without enthusiasm—but when the end comes there will be an irrevocable end to such tolerance.

When John tells us that the dead bodies of two witnesses will lie unburied in the streets of the anti-Christian world-city (Rev. 11), he means to inform us in a symbolic way that this city will be built upon the ruins of the church and its mission in the world. This is not to say that there will be no believers left, but the church as an institution will have ceased to exist.

These are somber prophecies. Yet they are not intended to give rise to a defeatist attitude. We know that our church buildings will not remain standing. If they're used at all, it will be as dance halls and movie theatres. But as long as we are still allowed to use the church buildings for our purposes, we must use them so well that we and our children will be able to get along without them when the great oppression covers the world.

In Proverbs the sluggard is advised to follow the example of the industrious ant. It seems to me that the entire Christian church would do well to take a lesson from the ant—especially those members of the church who are even busier than ants when it comes to making a living.

26

The Final Outcome

> "No hand intervening, [he] shall himself be broken.
> This explanation of the vision of the mornings and
> the evenings is true, but you must keep the vision
> secret, for there are still many days to go."
> At this I, Daniel, lost consciousness; I was ill for
> several days. Then I got up to discharge my duties in
> the king's service, keeping the vision a secret, and not
> understanding what it meant (8:25-7 JB).

DANIEL'S VISION OF THE THINGS to come has shown us that the Antichrist will have virtually a free hand on earth. On the one hand he will be able to build his empire on the ruins of the old order, which will commit suicide through a massive war of destruction. On the other hand, the church, against which he will direct his most important attack, will be greatly weakened in advance through a falling away. Traders will play a major role in the assault on Zion's fortress made by the gates of hell. Jesus alluded to this when He said that many will fall away and *betray* one another (Matt. 24:10).

The reign of the Antichrist will be short but gruesome, as Daniel 8 shows us. The prophet hears an angel ask how long the time of the persecution, in which the holy things are trampled underfoot and worship is made impossible because of the elimination of the "continual burnt offering," will last (8:13).

This question is not hard to understand. Jesus Himself said that if the time were not shortened, not a faithful believer would be left at the end. We're also told that the souls under the altar ask: "Holy, faithful Master, how much longer will you wait before you pass sentence and take vengeance for our death on the inhabitants of the earth?" (Rev. 6:10 NEB).

The mysterious answer to this question is given to us in the book of Daniel: "For two thousand three hundred evenings and mornings; then the holy place shall emerge victorious" (8:14 NEB). Later Daniel is assured: "This revelation which has been given of the evenings and mornings is true" (vs. 26 NEB).

Those 2,300 nights will include many painful, lonely hours for the watchmen. The hours will drag by agonizingly slowly as the watchmen long and pray for morning.

Here again we must resist the impulse to figure out exactly how long the oppression of the church will last. In such prophetic books as Daniel and the Revelation to John, numbers often have a symbolic meaning. The main point is that the numbers are given to us in thousands and hundreds—2300 evenings and mornings.

What this number is intended to suggest is that this period represents a considerable stretch of time, and that the measure must be full before the end can come. On the other hand, this text also shows us that our days and nights are counted individually in heaven. God does not forget His suffering people. He checks off each day on the calendar of world history. More than anyone else, He himself longs for the end.

It is without reason that the Bible speaks here of evenings and mornings rather than of days, for each evening and morning a burnt offering is to be lit in the temple. When this worship is interrupted, God's name is dishonored. The duration of the oppression is limited to those 2300 mornings and evenings even more for the sake of His name than out of consideration for the church.

There is a fearful period in store for the church, then. No more sacrifices will be lit in public worship services, just as there was no public worship when the church was forced to flee into the catacombs. The only religion tolerated will be the worship of man himself—ultimately, the worship of the beast. All believers who still dare to confess the name of the

Lord will be subjected to a devilish boycott. But God will be counting the days. If He preserves the tears of the church in a jar, won't He also keep careful track of those 2300 evenings and mornings?

It's hard to say how many kingdoms there will be before the kingdom of the Antichrist. But one thing we do know: his kingdom will be the last one—or rather, the second last one. The last and eternal kingdom, which is at the same time the first kingdom, is the Kingdom of God. In the final struggle Christ will be the Victor. His Kingdom is the Kingdom of all ages.

What will happen at the end of time is communicated to us in these words: "By no human hand, he shall be broken" (8:25). The hand that will break the Antichrist is God's hand, the hand that controls all things, the hand that wrote "Mene, Tekel" on Belshazzar's wall, the hand in which all the threads of history come together.

In a certain sense this prophecy has already been fulfilled. The one who will be broken without the intervention of any human hand is in the first place Antiochus Epiphanes, the hater of the Jewish religion and the forerunner of the Antichrist. One day, when this man of the sword was out on a military campaign bent on making some new conquest, he was struck down unexpectedly by a mysterious disease that led to his death. This disease seems to have been a form of madness. It's only a short step, then, from the sadistic excess of a despot to complete insanity! God's hand can certainly be seen in this incident.

God will not tolerate people laughing at Him. It may be true for a while that the godless enjoy success, but in the end, they will be broken! This is the continual refrain in this Daniel 8: broken horns and broken kingdoms. Only of God's Word and His Kingdom can it be said that they will not be broken. The glorious crown will rest eternally on the head of David's great Son.

The Antichrist will suffer the same fate as Antiochus Epiphanes. Just when his power reaches its zenith, he will be broken—but not by any human hand. There will be no one on earth with sufficient power to overthrow this dictator. He will be overthrown only when the cry, "Maranatha! Jesus is coming!" is at last heard around the world.

Jesus' appearance on the scene will come as a horrifying surprise to the Antichrist, just as Antiochus was taken by surprise when he was struck down by his mysterious illness. At the point when all the world bows in reverential awe before the Antichrist, the curtains of heaven will open, and Christ will return to the earth to settle all scores and judge mankind!

God's church will enjoy a glorious restoration on that day! The new Jerusalem will descend from heaven. The mountains will be bearers of peace, in the hills will be ambassadors of holy righteousness. Then the continual burnt offering of thanksgiving will burn continually on God's altar.

Let's be sure we realize what that day will bring: in the restored, renewed world, there will be place only for people who have been renewed to the depths of their being by God's Spirit, that is, people in whom His image has been restored. This does not mean that believers must already be perfect before death, for even the holiest of mortals manage only a small beginning in obedience. But it does mean that there must be solid evidence of a new direction in our lives.

Perhaps I express this point better by borrowing a metaphor from chapter 8 of Daniel. The unbelieving world is presented as a ram and as a he-goat with powerful horns. But the believer can better be symbolized by a sheep, a sheep that often goes astray but still follows the voice of the Good Shepherd. The believer is to resemble the Lamb of God, who did not open His mouth in protest when He was marked and uttered no threats when He suffered.

The believing attitude that the church must assume in the dark days ahead is described for us in greater detail through the response of Daniel when he received the revelation recorded in the eighth chapter. Three things are told to us. First Daniel was instructed: "Keep the vision secret, for there are still many days to go." What this means is that Daniel was to preserve the vision or revelation very carefully, just as a valuable document is safeguarded in an archive.

The reason for this is that there are still "many days to go"; it may still be quite some time before this or that element of the prophecy is fulfilled. Yet, when it does happen, it will be unmistakable. Then we will be able to see that God's Word predicted all of it in detail long in advance. This is what gives us special encouragement in this chapter.

It is certainly fortunate that the Bible has been preserved by God through all the ages despite the efforts of its enemies, and that this vision of Daniel has been preserved with it. Therefore, these events will not catch us entirely unprepared; there is no need for us to be surprised at the things to come. We know just what were in for. We know what to expect—from the world and from God.

Thus, we must turn to the Scriptures daily. We should read them faithfully and preserve them as carefully as our most costly possessions. Hold fast to the scriptures and savor them one by one. The Word of the Lord will stand forever!

Earlier I mentioned that Daniel was to preserve these words just as carefully as one safeguards a valuable document in an archive. Of course, this is not to suggest that the Bible is a literary relic of ancient times that belongs in an archive, or that we should treat it as an antique—which is indeed what many people do. Daniel's response to these revelations is a strong protest against the very thought of locking the revelation away in a safety deposit box: "At this I, Daniel, lost consciousness."

Obviously, Daniel did not react the way some people do when they read the Bible or hear a sermon preached, that is, by shrugging their shoulders and going their own way just as if nothing had happened. God's message overwhelms Daniel. His reaction to it even affected his body, for he was ill for several days afterward.

This does not mean that we must become physically ill in response to God's Word. But it does mean that the Word should not leave us unmoved. That Word should never give us a moment's peace—but in another sense it should give us peace all the time, a peace that passes understanding.

Daniel's reaction was a consequence of his intense concern with the fortunes of God's people. He had heard what was to happen to them; he was told all about the powerful horns. His soul cried out because of the misery His people would have to endure. He cried out even more because of the great falling away that would take place. This concern, especially, should drive us on the frightening days we live in, upsetting us and forcing us to pray, "Lord, have mercy on us!"

The third and last thing we are told about Daniel's response to this revelation is: "Then I got up to discharge my duties in the king's service, keeping the vision a secret, and not understanding what it meant." The prophet was disturbed by the vision, but he was not shattered. He used his faith to regain control of himself, and he returned to the king's service. Anyone who lives by faith in God does not let his anxieties dominate his life and does not fall into despair—not even when he is suffering greatly or facing inescapable turmoil.

"I got up to discharge my duties in the king's service." This should also be our watchword today. However confining our circumstances, however much we may grieve at the losses we have suffered; the King's work must go ahead. Our King's cause advances in spite of and through all that warfare and suffering.

We're approaching the final outcome. Will you and I be on the winning side? Of one thing we can be sure: Christ will be the Victor!

27

Come, Lord Jesus!

*O Lord, hear; O Lord, forgive; O Lord, listen and
act; for thy own sake do not delay, O God
(9:19 NEB).*

WE HAVE NOW ARRIVED at the ninth chapter of the book of Daniel, more than half of which is devoted to Daniel's prayer. Studying this prayer would do us some good. After all, who would not turn to prayer in such horrible, frightening times? We would do well to read through this lengthy prayer carefully and immerse ourselves in Daniel's situation.

Here Daniel makes himself a spokesman for a nation of sinners. His time was a fearful time, for the people of the Lord were in exile and Jerusalem lay in ruins. The chosen people felt the heavy hand of the oppressor.

When Daniel sends up a prayer to God in his people's hour of need, he does not lay the blame at the door of the proud, powerful, godless Babylonians. In his prayer there is no trace of indignation at the idea of a mighty power trampling a small nation like Israel underfoot. On the contrary, Daniel manfully takes the full blame on himself and his people.

This whole chapter is a moving, humbling confession of guilt, and that's what should draw our attention particularly. In times of war and disaster, the question of guilt always arises. People point first to this one and then to that one as the guilty party. Like Daniel, we must learn to begin by pointing the finger of accusation at *ourselves*. If we don't do so, will never learn the lesson that Daniel 9 is intended to teach us, and then we'll never be able to join in Daniel's prayer—which is exactly the prayer we need to pray.

In our text for this chapter, Daniel's prayer reaches its culmination. In a few short sentences he expresses his need and desire: "O Lord, hear; O Lord, forgive; O Lord listen and act; for thy own sake do not delay." What is this desire that fills Daniel's soul? (It is not spelled out in the text, but the Lord knew perfectly well what Daniel was asking for.) Daniel's petition, we learn from the context, is for the restoration of Jerusalem.

We feel inclined to ask whether this petition may not have been superfluous, given the circumstances. The occasion for this prayer was that Daniel had read in the Scriptures (see

9:2) that Jerusalem would lie in ruins for 70 years. Isn't that amazing? Daniel actually read the Scriptures! (Apparently, he was reading the prophecy of Jeremiah.) Although Daniel had received a number of special revelations from God, he was not above studying the Scriptures to learn more about God's will.

What Daniel read in Jeremiah's prophecy was that Jerusalem would be rebuilt after 70 years. Of course, he had read that before, but on this occasion, it struck him in particular, for 68 of those 70 years had already gone by. Thus, Daniel was busy examining the events of his day in light of the Scriptures, trying to read the signs of the times. In the process he made the exhilarating discovery that "the end was near."

That's also how *we* should read the Scriptures. Then true excitement will be ours. Daniel now had reason to rejoice, for God would again extend His protection to Zion. The time of humiliation was drawing to a close for His holy city. The day of restoration for which Daniel had yearned so long was dawning. Therefore, Daniel prayed to God not to delay.

What would have been more natural than for Daniel to begin his preparations for departure now that he had made his joyful discovery? After all, he had it in black and white! Daniel had read it with his own eyes. The unfolding of events corresponded exactly to what Jeremiah had prophesied.

The strange thing is that this man of God went to his knees in prayer just as if there were no promise in Jeremiah's prophecy, as if everything was still dark around him—whereas in fact the sun of freedom was already rising. Daniel poured out his soul in a fiery petition, an urgent prayer in which the words did not issue from his mouth smoothly: "O Lord, hear; O Lord, forgive; O Lord, listen and act; for thy own sake do not delay."

Only someone who does not understand the ways of the Spirit of God would say that this prayer is superfluous and would fail to understand it. Prayers are always the ladder down which God makes His blessing descend on us from heaven. He wishes to give His gracious blessing only to those who empty their souls before Him in prayer and thank Him for His goodness. He puts His promise before us as something that is ours if we claim it in prayer.

Prayers are indispensable links to the chain of God's dealings with man. Just as a prayer means nothing without a promise, a promise means nothing without a prayer. Because of this simple fact alone, prayer was necessary. Daniel did not pray despite the promise but because of it.

We should not jump to the conclusion that Daniel begged the Lord not to delay because he doubted God's promise. He had heard the promise from God's own mouth; to him it was as sure as 2 plus 2 equals 4. No, it was not doubt that drove Daniel to prayer. If Daniel were in doubt, his prayer would not have been a sincere prayer, for someone who doubts as he prays is only as steady as a wave on the turbulent sea.

What drove Daniel to pray was a deep desire to make God's cause his own cause. We could translate Daniel's prayer for the restoration of Jerusalem into New Testament language as follows: "Come, Lord Jesus! Yes, come quickly!"

This outlook on prayer needs further explanation. In general, our prayer life goes smoothly—as long as we are praying for our own welfare. When it's a question of our material needs, our knees are not too stiff to bend in prayer. Then we are able to force the most moving petitions from our lips. But when the issue is *the Lord's cause*, we usually fall silent. Then we often become so spiritual as to adopt a wait-and-see attitude instead of joining in the struggle through prayer.

The beautiful thing about Daniel's prayer is that the issue at stake was the Lord's cause. Daniel himself had never been back to Jerusalem. Furthermore, he would hardly be advocating himself in the world by returning. He had a good position at the court, and a return to Jerusalem would bring him no material advantage.

But the prophet had his mind on higher things than wealth and power. He knew that the ruins of Jerusalem gave the heathens something to laugh about. They were laughing not so much at Israel as at Israel's God. They said, "What a feeble god! He can't even protect his own people!" This cut Daniel to the quick. Therefore, he begged the Lord to put an end to the mockery—not for Israel's sake but "for thy own sake, O God."

Thus, Daniel made the Lord's cause his own cause and prayed that the Lord would glorify Himself through the restoration of Jerusalem, thereby erasing the heathen insults to His name. What Daniel was asking for is exactly what will come about when Jesus restores His church, the New Testament Jerusalem, on the day of His return and crushes all His enemies. Therefore, the prayer of Daniel can indeed be read as an Old Testament version of John's petition, "Come, Lord Jesus!"

This brings us back to the need of our own time. We are here given a clear indication of what tensions ought to be present in our prayers.

From thousands of hearts in our own time, the same prayer arises to God: "O Lord, hear; O Lord, forgive; O Lord, listen and act; for thy own sake do not delay." What is it that God should grant immediately? I suppose most people think first of their own needs, of their own poor community and nation. We then beg the Lord to let us keep such rich blessings as peace, freedom, and independence.

There's nothing wrong with such prayers: such requests are made again and again in prayer. The point to remember is that there's more to prayer.

Let's not close our eyes to the fact that Christ is busy building the New Jerusalem, which is to be constructed according to God's specifications so that it will stand forever, by means of the tumult and talk of war. The birth of this new world, like every birth, will involve a good deal of pain. The structure that we call our earth is not just in need of remodeling; sin has done its work too thoroughly for that. Our earth must be leveled completely. That's why there are so many wars, rumors of wars, fires, and bloody disasters. In each blast of the cannon and each exploding shell, we hear a voice from heaven saying: "Jesus is coming!" God is making all things new.

Like Daniel, we can read this promise in "the Book." If we let the light of the prophetic Word shine on the events of the day, we, too, will declare the time is drawing near.

It's certain that all God's promises will be fulfilled. All the same, these promises should lead us to pray. We should pray for Jesus to come with His thousands of angels to glorify His name. At present the glory of Christ does not shine through. He has been given all power in heaven and on earth, but it often appears as though the power really belongs to the devil. Christ is the King of the ages, but at the moment His throne seems to be occupied by man, who is so small, yet so powerful and bold.

This is what should cause us the most pain of all, but it does not appear to have pained us very much so far. We are much too concerned with our own glory to worry about Christ's glory.

There is not enough force behind our prayers. The yearning for Christ's return does not live in our souls and remain uppermost in our minds. Perhaps the Lord has sent the unrest in our time in order to inject some urgency into our prayers. If so, we are gaining a great deal at the cost of only a small loss.

When God sends tribulation, the church triumphant in heaven and the militant church on earth will beg Him even harder in prayer for Christ's return. Even if answering that prayer means that various catastrophes must take place and that we ourselves must suffer because of them, we should continue to pray: "O Lord, hear; O Lord, forgive; O Lord, listen and act; *for thy own sake* do not delay."

28

A Humble Attitude

O Lord, hear; O Lord, forgive; O Lord, listen and act; for thy own sake do not delay, O God, for thy city and thy people bear thy name (9:19 NEB).

LET'S LOOK AT THIS PRAYER of Daniel once more. We have good reason to examine it carefully, for a prayer that rises from a believing heart is many-sided. Any other kind of prayer is impoverished, however rich it may be in words. The many-sidedness of this prayer comes out partially in that the prophet not only makes God's cause his own cause, as we saw in the previous chapter, but is also sure that God will make Jerusalem's cause His cause, as we shall see shortly.

What impresses us immediately about this prayer is Daniel's *humility*. If we are to pray as we ought to pray, if we are to please God with our prayers, if our prayers are to be heard, then we must not only pray with a proper awareness of our sin but must also humble ourselves before God's majesty. Knowing about our need and misery is not enough. The greatest need is not something external but something *internal*. The most basic of all questions is that of sin and guilt. There are many people who fail to humble themselves properly in prayer simply because they have forgotten this. On this point, too, we have much to learn from Daniel.

Daniel begins his prayer by saying, "O Lord, *forgive*!" Israel was in exile and had lost many precious possessions—home and jewelry, temple services and freedom. In such circumstances, what could be more natural than to pray, "O Lord, *give*—give us back our fields and homes, our temple and our city and our precious freedom"?

Daniel does the unexpected by praying, "O Lord, forgive." He does not begin by asking for *restoration* but begs the righteous Judge for *grace*. We do not hear him cry out, "Have mercy on us in the misery of our exile." Instead, he prays, "Have mercy on us in the misery of our *guilt*." The latter misery is much greater than all the hardships of exile, war, poverty, and sickness put together.

The prophet finds it impossible to begin with a request for the restoration of Jerusalem. The words stick in his throat. He feels he cannot begin with such a petition, for the rebuilding of the city and the temple is not to be taken for granted.

On the contrary, it would be a *miracle* if it were to happen, for Israel's guilt is unspeakably great.

Daniel does not find it strange, then, that not one stone was left upon another, that the Israelites were trampled underfoot by the proud conquerors, that the might of the wicked forced them into the misery of exile. "O my sin, my sin!" he laments. The man of God bows his head and cries from the depths, "O Lord, forgive!"

Thus, Daniel certainly has a deep, thorough knowledge of his need and misery. Anyone who cries without ceasing, "O Lord, give me this and give me that!" instead of, "O Lord, forgive!" does not know what it means to pray to God in troubled times.

Daniel's prayer also shows us how alike prophetic souls are. Consider Amos, for example. Perhaps you recall how Amos once had a vision of a great swarm of locusts coming down to devour the crops. He fell on his knees and begged, "O Lord God, forgive; what will Jacob be after this? He is so small" (Amos 7:2 NEB). If we had been in Amos's place, we would no doubt have prayed, "O Lord God, take all those locusts away and spare our fields, for it's a matter of life and death to us!" But that was not Amos' prayer. He prayed instead for forgiveness. Daniel and Amos and all who live in humble fear of the Lord know perfectly well that there are more serious dangers than locusts and greater privations than the loss of freedom. "O, my sin, my sin! O Lord, forgive!"

The humility of this prayer comes out in the second place in the fact that Daniel makes no attempt whatsoever to transfer the blame for the present misery to others. Certainly, that would have been easy enough to do. Weak, peace-loving nations are swallowed up by the powerful armies of belligerent nations. Consequently, the question of guilt can be settled quickly. Wasn't it the fault of those godless "might makes right" Babylonians that Israel had to spend year after year in the misery of exile? That's not how Daniel reasoned! "O Lord, the shame falls on us as on our kings, our princes and our forefathers; we have all sinned against thee" (9:8 NEB).

Isn't that an amazing, moving confession? Shoulder to shoulder with godless Babylon stands the equal godless but supposedly pious city of Jerusalem! The faithful covenant people, the members of the church, are the guilty ones! Now we begin to see what Daniel was up to when he prayed that strange, amazing prayer: "O Lord, forgive."

In the third place, Daniel's humility is apparent from the fact that he confesses his sins and the sins of his people without trying to minimize or gloss over anything. He can hardly find words strong enough to denounce the shamefulness of sin before God. "We have sinned and done wrong and acted wickedly and rebelled, turning aside from thy commandments and ordinances; we have not listened to thy servants the prophets, who spoke in thy name to our kings, our princes and our fathers, and to all the people of the land" (9:5-6).

This is not a meaningless string of hollow words but there's a description of the deadly advance of sin, an account of how things went from bad to worse. Sin led to injustice, injustice led to godlessness, and godlessness led to rebellion. Finally, there arose a feeling that God was the enemy. The evil was everywhere, in all segments of society. The king was just as guilty as the rest of the people.

The cause of all this misery was that Israel did not listen to God's servants, the prophets, who spoke in His name. Of course, the Israelites couldn't help hearing what these servants of the Lord said, whether they agreed or not. Sometimes they reacted favorably, and sometimes critically, depending largely on their mood. Yet they seemed to have no idea that these prophets actually spoke in the name of the Lord, that they came with an authoritative message— "Thus says the Lord."

The Israelites heard, but they did not listen. They let the prophets talk, but they refused to take them seriously. They went on living just as before. They remained just as cold and covetous and worldly and materialistic and hateful as they had always been. They made much of this and that, founding organisations and starting projects. But the result was whited sepulchers containing nothing but the rotten bones of the dead. Yet that didn't deter them. They quarrelled about covenant faithfulness and self-examination—but neglected both of them. That—and a great deal more besides—was their sin. That was the sin they had to learn to confess in concrete terms—with Daniel.

Confessing one's guilt in general without specifying that this was wrong and that was sinful is both cheap and meaningless. Without specific confession, everything stays as it is, even after God sends a hurricane to sweep across the land and through the churches. "O, my sin, my sin! O Lord forgive!"

What distinguishes us from the world is not that we are less wicked but that by the grace of God we have learned to see our wickedness for what it is and that we confess our sins. The church is the only body on earth that confesses sin. Where the confession of sins dies out, the church is no longer church.

At the beginning of the Second World War, Neville Chamberlain, the British Prime Minister, declared that the responsibility for the catastrophe engulfing Europe rested on the shoulders of one man—Adolf Hitler. His statement was greeted with loud applause, of course, for that's the kind of language we like to hear. But anyone in a right relationship to God does not cheer when he hears such language. Instead, he cries out with the statesman and the prophet Daniel, "O Lord, this shame falls on us!"

If such an awareness does not permeate the minds of rulers and kings, of statesmen and cabinet ministers, there will be no new dawn for this battered world—unless God should see fit to spare Sodom for the sake of ten righteous people in our time. Let's hope He'll be able to find ten. And let's hope, too, that the church really will confess its guilt.

If only we would stand next to the man supposedly responsible for the mess we're in and say, "I share the responsibility!" After all, what have *we* done with God's benefits, with all those answered prayers, with God's great patience towards us? We have squandered what God has given us! "O, my sin, my sin! O Lord, forgive!"

Once Daniel had begged God to forgive Israel's great guilt, he could go further and ask that the Israelites be delivered from exile and that the city, and the temple of God be restored. That required great faith, for at the time there was nothing to be seen but smoking ruins. Daniel achieved a breakthrough in his prayer and stood firm in the conviction that Jerusalem would one day rise again in its full beauty.

How could he be so sure of this? He was certain of it because he was convinced that God would make Jerusalem's cause His own cause, that He would regard the restoration of Jerusalem as a matter of His own honor. Daniel argued in prayer: "Thy city and thy people bear thy name." In other words: "It's up to You, Lord. If Your people do not regain their freedom and Your city remains a pile of ruins, what will remain of Your great name? What will the heathens say then—not about us but You?" With that argument Daniel made it clear that it was *God's* move. *God* was the one to take the initiative. Even if God were concerned with nothing but His own glory, this prayer could not remain unanswered. There is no higher appeal in prayer than the appeal to God's own honor!

Jerusalem's situation must not be identified with the plight in which the nations now find themselves. What we read here in Daniel cannot be applied directly to our time. All we know is that God loves the right and will see to it that justice triumphs in the end. He makes the cause of the righteous His own.

Whether we will see all of this with our own eyes is another question. Time will tell. But we don't need to fear that satan will somehow snatch us from Christ's hand. However dark God's ways may be, now and in the future, He will surely protect us.

He does not protect us because we are so precious in ourselves. After all, what do we amount to? We're a lost cause, a hopeless case. But we do have one assurance to cling to: we bear *God's name* on our foreheads, which baptism symbolizes by the sprinkling of water. We and our children bear God's name, and therefore our safety and welfare is God's concern—in times of high prices and in times of famine.

Indeed, God has given us the assurance that He will provide us with all good things and keep evil away from us or turn it to our profit. We can count on this promise; it's as certain as 2 plus 2 equals 4. Again and again the earthly losses of believers have been translated into great spiritual gains. Even if we have not seen this in our own lives as yet, we must believe it!

We are on firm ground, then, when we bring up the issue of God's honor as we pray to Him. After all, we do bear His name. We can perish only if He perishes! Clinging to this knowledge in faith, we sing that even in times of peril our hearts are at peace in the Lord.

29

In God's Inner Chamber

He said then, "Daniel, do not be afraid: from that first day when you resolve to humble yourself before God, the better to understand, your words have been heard; and your words are the reason why I have come. The prince of the kingdom of Persia has been resisting me for twenty-one days (10:12-13 JB).

WE NOW MOVE ON to the third year of the reign of Cyrus, king of Persia, as we learn from the first verses of Daniel 10. Now, it might appear strange that Daniel is still at the foreign court and not in Jerusalem, for you recall that Cyrus, in the first year of his reign, gave the Jews permission to go back to Palestine. Naturally many Jews jumped at the chance and returned to their homeland joyfully. "If I forget you, O Jerusalem, let my right-hand wither away" (Ps. 137:5 NEB).

Daniel's decision to remain at the Persian court is not to be explained on the basis of any indifference towards the land of his fathers. We remember well from his prayer in Chapter 9 how much his soul yearned for the city of the Great King.

There is only one conceivable reason for his decision to stay behind, a reason not revealed to us expressly in the text. We must assume that God had made it clear to him in some way or other that he was not to leave his post. Speaking in human terms, we might say that God could not do without Daniel yet, that there was still a task for him in the land of exile.

When we are shown that there is still work for us to do, we try to suppress our own desires and selfish impulses in order to give unconditional obedience to God's will, which alone is good. At least, that's what we do if the third petition of the Lord's Prayer is more than a mere phrase to us.

In this case, too, it is clear that only God's will is good. It was fortunate that God left Daniel in the land of exile, for although king Cyrus was favorably disposed toward the Jews, all sorts of hostile powers were hard at work, both openly and secretly (as we learn from the book of Ezra). These enemies of the Jews tried to stir up the Persian court and the king. In various insidious ways, those who were hostile to the Jews tried to prevent the rebuilding of the city and the temple.

God had so arranged things that the Jews had someone to plead their case before the king—Daniel. But that's not all. Daniel did not plead the cause of God's people only before the king of Persia; he also interceded on their behalf before the King of kings in heaven. In other words, Daniel was a man of prayer. Such a man is worth as much as a thousand fighting heroes—if not more. In any event, Daniel could do as much for the Lord's cause while remaining at his post in Persia as the man who stood on Jerusalem's wall with a sword in one hand and a trowel in the other.

In an army, every soldier has his place. An army can't get by with combat troops alone; it also needs personnel to look after the food and supplies. Furthermore, officers are needed to plan the attack. Finally, an army needs fathers and mothers, that is, people who stay home and pray for God's blessing. Actually, I should have put the last category first. Let no one think—especially the infirmed and aged—that he can be of no use in the great struggle to establish God's Kingdom. Each of us has access to the Court of courts. We are allowed to plead the cause of God's people before the One who controls everything.

As we shall see, Daniel's prayers succeeded in drawing angels from heaven to earth. These angels formed an invincible heavenly guard around the people of the Lord, with the result that the plans of the enemy failed. In the mighty battle then being fought between the Kingdom of God and the kingdom of this world, Daniel succeeded in mobilizing the angels as a spiritual air force against the satanic powers in the air. We will hear more about this later when we consider this 21-day battle of the angels against the prince of the kingdom of Persia, the battle mentioned in our text for the next chapter.

We now turn to the words with which our text begins: "Fear not, Daniel, for from the first day that you set your mind to understand and humbled yourself before your God, your words have been heard, and I have come because of your words" (10:12).

This reassurance by the angel contains a powerful message. To view it in the proper perspective, we must go back to the beginning of the chapter. There Daniel tells us that he mourned and fasted for three weeks. We hardly need guess at his reason for doing so; the angel reminds us that Daniel had set his mind to *understand* and had *humbled* himself before God.

Daniel wanted to understand what the future would bring for his poor people. He was not at ease about this question, for he had seen how various enemies were working against God's purposes. Sometimes he wondered anxiously whether the battle would be won or lost.

The important thing to note is that Daniel *humbled* himself as he sought to understand. This indicates that he did more than just worry about things. He knew that prayer was the only answer, and therefore he began to pray.

When the angel declared that Daniel's words had been heard in heaven on the first day of his fast, he meant his words of prayer. The complaints we mutter under our breath or even direct towards others do not reach heaven. But words spoken in prayer go a long way: they are heard by God Himself!

Such were the words that the prophet spoke. He didn't pray just for a few minutes; he prayed without ceasing. His tongue never tired of speaking, and his hand never tired of knocking on heaven's door. He mourned and fasted for three weeks—21 days straight!

After those 21 days, an angel appeared to him. This happened when he was making a trip with a group of people. He found himself on the bank of the Tigris River, which like the Euphrates, is one of the great rivers of Mesopotamia (10:4-5).

There is a direct connection between Daniel's prayer and the appearance of the angel. The angel himself said: "I have come because of your words." Thus, it was Daniel's prayer that brought this angel down from heaven, just as an angel appeared to release Peter from prison when the church in Jerusalem prayed for him. The power of prayer is so immense that it can even call angels down to earth to help God's people.

The face of this angel was like the appearance of lightning (10:6). His presence caused a panic among Daniel's friends: they were terrified and ran away to hide (vs. 7). If the angel had this effect on Daniel's *friends*, just imagine how it could terrify his *enemies!* When God rushes to the side of His beleaguered people with his air force of angels, the help he offers has a devastating effect and certainly gets the job done.

In addition to his unnamed angel, we are told that Michael, who is "one of the chief princes" (10:13) and the commander of the heavenly hosts, was to join in the battle. We know Michael especially from the Book of Revelation, where he appears as a hero engaged in a great battle with the dragon. Thus, heavenly powers rushed to Daniel's assistance as God's answer to his prayer.

All the same, there is something mysterious about this story. The air force of angels did come to the assistance of Daniel and his countrymen—but they seem to have taken their time. Twenty-one days is a long time to wait, but that's how long Daniel waited before the angel appeared before his amazed eyes. By that time everything could have been lost! Daniel had to wait three weeks—despite the fact that his cry for help had reached God's ears on the very first day, as the angel himself emphasized.

Let's take a close look at these two facts: the prayer was heard on the first day, but this only became apparent to Daniel after three weeks. Here the angel, speaking to Daniel, gives us an interesting look into God's inner chamber. "From the first day your words have been heard." This shows us how quickly things happen when it comes to prayer. God does not favor certain persons over others. Therefore, we can rest assured that our prayers are heard just as quickly as Daniel's prayers were. What a surprise!

It's not that God will eventually hear us if only we go on praying long enough. From the very first instant, the hearer of prayers gives His full attention to our petition. That's quick service, wouldn't you say? But the Bible tells us that it can go even faster, that God sometimes answers us even before we call out to Him. God knows what we need even before we address Him in prayer. Hence it could almost be said that prayers are answered five minutes before they are sent up.

But if this is so, the incident involving Daniel becomes twice as mysterious. Why did Daniel have to wait three weeks before finding out that his prayer was being answered? All this time he was unaware that God had heard his voice. Day after day passed by—21 of them in a row—while Daniel saw no light whatsoever. There seemed to be no one to hear his prayer and respond. All this time the prophet sat mourning in sackcloth and ashes.

If Daniel had not been a believer, he might have concluded that there was no God in heaven and that all his praying was a waste of time. But Daniel had not been praying in vain, as we shall soon see.

At this point it becomes quite clear that God sometimes makes us wait for a while before we see an answer to our prayers. We may have to wait for 21 days, which really isn't all that long. We may even have to wait for 21 *years*. Sometimes we never see an answer to our prayers with our own eyes.

The prayer we raise may well be answered and the answer may become fully apparent after our death because God for some reason or other does not regard it as necessary for us to see it.

The main thing, in any event, is not seeing but *believing*. "Blessed are those who have not seen and yet believe" (John 20:29). Even if I had *never* seen an answer to prayer—and I doubt whether there is any believer who could say that—I would still believe that God hears the prayers sent to Him. One of the reasons that Daniel 10 is in the Bible is to teach us this lesson. This chapter shows us that God is immediately busy with His response to our prayers—even if only in a provisional manner that we cannot see yet.

Consider the story told by this amazing angel. As a result of Daniel's prayer, the angel was commanded on the very first day to go to the earth. "I have come because of your words." It's almost as though he were apologizing to Daniel for not appearing earlier. The reason, he explains to Daniel, is that the "prince of the kingdom of Persia withstood me twenty-one days." We will see in the next chapter who this Persian prince was. For the present, suffice it to say that he was one of satan's lieutenants.

The intermediate period, in which Daniel seemed to be waiting in vain for an answer to his prayer, had been well used by the angel: he was engaged in a battle with devils. Behind the curtain of clouds, a mighty but invisible battle was fought between the Angel of light and the prince of darkness. In fighting this battle, the angel was doing exactly what was necessary as an answer to Daniel's prayer. Daniel had asked that the attacks of the evil one, who sought to stir up the king and the other rulers against the Jews, be halted so that the heart of the king might be won for the cause of the Jews. God granted this request by sending angels who put the devils to flight.

The Lord responded on the very first day—but Daniel had no way of knowing this. Faith, we must remember, is also the conviction of things not seen.

30

In the Devil's Headquarters

*The prince of the kingdom of Persia withstood
me twenty-one days (10:13).*

AS SOON AS DANIEL'S PRAYER for the welfare of Jerusalem reached heaven, the angel who eventually appeared to Daniel and spoke to him was commanded to go to the earth. Through the intervention of a heavenly air force, the demonic dangers that now threatened Israel would be beaten back.

Why the angel did not appear to Daniel until 21 days had passed, why the prophet found out only then that his prayers had been heard in heaven and answered, is now explained by the messenger from heaven: "The prince of the kingdom of Persia withstood me twenty-one days." This was the lawful reason for the delay. Actually, I shouldn't call it a delay at all, for the three-week battle between the angel of God and the prince of the kingdom of Persia had brought about just what Daniel had prayed for so fervently.

Who was this mysterious prince of the kingdom of Persia whom the angel found standing in his way? He was clearly an antagonist of the heavenly figure with whom Daniel spoke. Since God's angels are spirits, we may take it that this Persian prince was not a man of flesh and blood either but some sort of spiritual power, more specifically, an evil spiritual power. Thus, the angel was speaking about a devil.

It should come as no surprise that this evil spirit is given the title of prince—the prince of the kingdom of Persia. Devils are fallen powers, but they are still forces to be reckoned with. They are able to take control and are not to be taken lightly. In Jude's epistle we read: "Not even the archangel Michael, when he was engaged in argument with the devil about the corpse of Moses, dared to denounce him in the language of abuse" (vs. 9 JB). Paul manifests the same weary respect when he speaks of the spiritual hosts of wickedness as principalities and powers. Thus, the devils are princes indeed; there is something royal about them. Yet we could better speak of them as tyrants and usurpers.

The prince mentioned by the angel is one of the rulers of the kingdom of darkness. He is introduced as "the prince of the kingdom of Persia." Later we hear of another devil, who is called "the prince of Greece." The angel says to Daniel: "I am first going back to fight with the prince of Persia, and as soon as I have left, the prince of Greece will appear" (10:20 NEB).

Satan, who is the commander in chief of the kingdom of darkness, is an outstanding organizer. Nothing is left to chance in the great war he wages against the church. Everything is planned, right down to the smallest detail. He has a number of assistants who are far more cunning than even the most clever human diplomats. We could perhaps call them the devil's fifth column. Each one of them is assigned to a particular country, to be an evil influence on its people through lies, propaganda, and other means, with the overall goal of stirring up hatred of the church of the Lord.

The subordinate devil who was assigned to Persia as his sphere of operations has been given the specific task of turning the Persian court against the Jews. He was the one at work behind the scenes in this chapter. Hence, he is called the prince of the kingdom of Persia. He was under satan's direct command and was personally responsible to him. That's why I have entitled this chapter "In the Devil's Headquarters."

The Scriptures do not hide things from us, nor do they leave us ignorant of satan's mode of operation. In the spiritual struggle we wage, we can never say that we were overcome by a spiritual attack. The curtain that separates us from the unseen world of spirits is here pulled aside for a moment as we are given a glimpse of a titanic struggle of spirits, a struggle that goes on all around us, even though we do not see it with our own eyes. What I mean, of course, is the struggle of the angels against the spiritual powers in the air.

Behind this struggle carried on in Jerusalem with the trowel and the sword was a struggle of spirits, a mighty battle between demons and angels. As soon as the spirits enter a battle, the fighting becomes even fiercer. This is also evident in our time. When animals are locked in combat, all they are able to throw into the struggle is physical strength, but when human beings wage war against each other, they use their sophisticated minds to develop such refined and effective weapons that welfare becomes hell on earth. The power of the mind makes the horror of war ten times as great.

I could also start talking about such spiritual forces as the propaganda and lies that the modern spiritual powers in the air used to poison our minds by way of radio and television. Propaganda has become a virtually indispensable tool in modern warfare. No one can rightly doubt the power of the mind.

Of course, no war would be possible if the government headquarters of the great powers were not first occupied by demonic forces. To put it in Daniel's language, no war would be waged if the princes of the various countries had not first blinded the statesmen. Satan, too, knows how to use the power of the mind. That's why he sent one of his generals to Persia—equipped not with an army or navy but simply with evil thoughts. His mission, as we have seen, was to stir up the Persian people and court against the Jews.

Thus, there were demonic forces behind the opposition of the Samaritans in Palestine. The Samaritans did everything they could to make things difficult for the Jews who had returned from exile. Various plots and conspiracies were concocted to hold back the coming of God's Kingdom. That was the work of the prince of the kingdom of Persia.

The prince of Greece, whom I mentioned earlier, was to go about his work in a much more refined way. His most effective weapon would be cunning. He would try to wipe out the Jewish people by enticing them to trade in the religion of their fathers for Greek culture and the Greek way of life. He would slay his ten thousands by encouraging conformity to the world.

The air inhaled by the Israelites was full of satanic forces and spirits that did not seek to destroy them with bombs but sought to capture their hearts. There were indeed spiritual powers in the air. Yet there was more in the air than wicked spiritual powers, propaganda, jet fighters, and bombers. The air was also filled with *angels*. In that anxious hour when Israel was under heavy attack from the air, the Lord's angels descended from heaven to do battle with the prince of Persia and the prince of Greece, taking the side of the people of the Lord.

This does not mean that these angels fought against the demons in the same way that an angel of the Lord once slaughtered thousands upon thousands of soldiers of Sennacherib. The battles fought were not physical, observable struggles between angels and demons. What happened is that the angels succeeded in blocking the influence of the demons. They managed to arrange things so that Persia's statesmen did not listen to the devils but instead took a favorable attitude toward the Jews. That this was indeed the outcome of the angels' effort is evident from the actual outcome.

It has often been said that the great battles of our time would be fought in the *air*. There is a good deal of truth to this, for man is making ever greater use of the air. He builds planes and missiles to fly through the air and sends propaganda, which is a significant part of any war effort, through the air. The church of the Lord should take this truth to heart, so that the children of light may become just as adept at using the air as children of darkness.

Let's not forget that Daniel's prayer ascended to heaven through the air and the clouds, and that the angels descended through the air to do battle with evil spiritual powers and to influence the Persian rulers. We, too, must use the air when we intercede with God for this unhappy world. Prayer mobilizes the forces of heaven against the forces of hell. Through prayer, the powers of wickedness, hatred, brutality, and injustice are broken.

Finally, we must not assume that the prince of Persia and Greece were the only demonic powers. Devils have not only been sent to Washington, Moscow, and Peking but also to Jerusalem. They can certainly be an evil influence on the church and the people of the Lord. Sometimes they take possession of our homes and our hearts, persuading us to set up our own ego as lord, encouraging us to put our own desires before all else and never to deny ourselves.

When this happens, the princes of darkness become our rulers, and Jesus is deposed from His throne. Therefore, we must pray for a mobilization of heaven's spiritual powers so that we will not succumb in this spiritual struggle but will be able to resist until we finally gain the upper hand.

Yes, without any false boasting we can declare that the final victory will be ours—or rather, that it will be Christ's. The battle will ultimately be won in the air. Before the horror-stricken eyes of the world, the heavens will open, and the Son of man will return on the clouds to judge everyone on earth.

The earth and its fullness belong to the Lord. This earth will be inherited not by those who rely on force but by those who are meek and gentle in spirit. All the devils will then be disposed of for good: they will be cast into the lake of fire. Then there will be no other sound in the air than the song of the angels, in which the voices of all the redeemed will join as they sing praises to God.

31

Before the Antichrist

In his place shall arise a contemptible person to whom royal majesty has not been given; he shall come in without warning and obtain the kingdom by flatteries (11:21).

WE LISTEN MOST ATTENTIVELY when we hear the screaming sirens alerting us to disaster all around us in our time. In the church the question arises whether the wars threatening the nations and the earthquakes tearing open the earth's crust are indications that the end has come, and that Christ is about to return. After all, the Lord Jesus did tell us that all these things are *signs* of His return. Yet He made a point of adding that these wars and afflictions are no more than a *beginning* of the torment yet to come.

Of course, this does not mean that we may continue to push the return of Christ into a vague, distant future, for these developments succeed each other so rapidly that the Lord will in fact appear unexpectedly, despite all the indications that the end is near. But it *does* mean that we should not expect the great day to dawn tomorrow, so to speak, for there are many things that must happen first.

In one of his letters, Paul makes it clear that the day of the Lord will not come until the man of sin, the son of perdition, has appeared (II Thess. 2). Before Jesus comes again to rule the new earth in righteousness, the nations and especially the church will have to endure a period of terror under the dominion of the "man of sin," whom we normally refer to as the Antichrist. What we look for, then, is not just an anti-Christian spirit or a godless outlook that will gradually gain the upper hand in the world but a person of flesh and blood.

This Antichrist will bear a certain perverse resemblance to Jesus Christ: he will be the exact opposite. Christ is the son of God, whereas the Antichrist is the son of perdition. Christ came to save, whereas the Antichrist comes to destroy.

Just as Christ was foreshadowed in the Old Testament by various figures whose lives reflected something of what He Himself would be, there was also a prefiguration of the Antichrist. Because the overwhelming glory of Christ could not be adequately foreshadowed in any one person, there were many prefigurations of Christ. Melchizedek, Joseph, Sampson, Solomon, David, and various others, even when taken together, constitute only a weak reflection of the many-sided majesty of the Son of Man.

But the Antichrist, by contrast, can be properly foreshadowed by a single forerunner. That forerunner was the Seleucid king Antiochus Epiphanes IV, the great enemy and persecutor of the Jews who lived about 160 years before Christ. This king was guilty of abominable desecration. It is his portrait that this chapter of Daniel sketches for us. Not only did the Holy Spirit predict his coming, He provided an accurate description of him so that the church would be able to recognize him immediately when he appeared. What the Antichrist will look like, how he will make his appearance on the stage, and how he will meet his end is revealed to us by way of Antiochus, who mirrors him so well.

This sketch actually begins with Daniel 11:21. The twenty verses preceding it are a description of the period *before* the Antichrist. It tells us about the events preparing the way for his appearance. This period before the Antichrist is our concern in this chapter.

To follow and comprehend the events related to us in the first 20 verses of Daniel 11 is certainly not easy. The passage as a whole is confusing. What it describes could be summarized as a story of rise and fall, of blood and tears, of wars and rumors of wars. The names of virtually all the great powers of that time (Persia, Greece, Egypt, and Syria) come up in this passage in an open or disguised way. We read of clashes between kings of the South (Egypt) and the north (Syria), with Palestine caught between the two as a sort of buffer state. We read of kings who send powerful armies into the field; and of other, more powerful kings who then destroy them. The one king attacks the other, sacrificing the lives of tens of thousands of soldiers (11:12), but the king who is attacked soon gets his revenge. We read of walls and fortifications and well defended cities (vs. 15) as well as of revolutions that fail (vs. 14). Furthermore, when the power of the armies is not sufficient, the kings resort to tricks and cunning: they seek to extend their power through marriages that establish bonds between royal families (vs. 17).

Things go on and on this way. The sea is exceedingly turbulent, as the waves break against each other. The sea foams and surges. Armies and navies, power and cunning, might and honor and esteem are all involved in the struggle, as everything whirls about, and the entire world is in a confused uproar.

That's what things look like in the world just before the appearance of the tyrant Antiochus. It went just as the angel had prophesied to Daniel, as anyone can see for himself by reading the history of that era. The prophecy of this chapter is historical, and it was fulfilled in the struggle between Persia, Greece, Egypt, and Syria for the dominance of the ancient world.

We must not misuse a chapter like Daniel 11 by reading it as a prophecy about the struggles and conflicts of our time. We may not play ingenious games with the Bible. Any effort to read this chapter as a prophecy about our time is doomed to failure.

Yet there is more in this passage then mere history! Just as there were wars and rumors of wars before Antiochus, that hater of religion, appeared on the scene, Daniel wants to teach us that the period before the reign of the Antichrist will also be a sorry time of blood and tears. The Antichrist will wade into the picture through a river of blood. Before he appears, the air will be filled with the sound of warfare, the cries of the tormented, and the wails of the mourners. This is the perspective from which the scriptures view the earthly uproar and chaos. Yet we must be careful not to deduce too much from the individual details in this chapter.

Modern man's hope is that after all the blood has been shed, the human race will finally come to its senses and never wage war again. But Daniel now shows us that this is a mere dream, for the most horrible things of all will follow the period of great warfare.

The "contemptible person" mentioned in our text for this chapter (the Antichrist, as we shall see) will come quietly and without warning to take control of one kingdom after the other. But that's only a beginning for him. Later he will launch an offensive against the rest of the world, using his armies and naval forces (11:40). Like a whirlwind, he will sweep away anything that stands in his path. He will seize the Holy Land and desecrate holy places, abolishing the perpetual sacrifice and replacing it with an unnamed abomination.

What was prophesied in Daniel 11 has already been fulfilled in part. Antiochus Epiphanes, about whom Daniel was talking in the first place, subjected the Jews to such horrible persecution that they could pray:

> God, the pagans have invaded your heritage,
> they have desecrated your holy Temple;
> they have reduced Jerusalem to a pile of ruins,
> they have left the corpses of your servants
> to the birds of the air for food,
> and the flesh of your devout to the beasts of the earth
> (Ps. 79:1-2 JB).

But this was only a pale reflection of the terrifying atrocities of the Antichrist. The scriptures confirm this in various places. Out of the turbulent sea of the nations, John sees the beast emerge as he tells us in the Book of Revelation. And Jesus told His disciples that when the great affliction comes, "they will hand you over to be tortured and put to death; and you will be hated by all the nations on account of my name" (Matt. 24:9 JB).

There's something about this period before the Antichrist that should draw our special attention. When we read the first half of Daniel 11, we see that it could well pass for a chapter in a book on world history, for it deals exclusively with the rise and fall of various powerful kingdoms. We may even scratch our heads and wonder why all this is recorded in the Bible. Isn't the Bible supposed to describe the history of God's Kingdom? Our surprise grows even greater when we note that nothing whatsoever is said about the church and the people of God.

All the same, this passage honors the church; it was not intended to simply tell us something about military history. That history, too, is *God's* history. These battles and accounts of the destinies of the nations would have no place in the Bible if they had nothing to do with the Kingdom of God. They do have a bearing on the Kingdom of God, just as the history of nations today has a bearing on the church.

What is the connection? Perhaps I could explain it as follows. In this passage we read about conflicts between the king of the north and the king of the south. Directly between the two territories lies the holy land. Therefore, the history related in this passage revolves around the holy land.

Now, the church is the midpoint of world history in more than a geographical sense. Everything hinges on the church. God ordains the events of history as part of His plan. Hence, He makes use of the powerful rulers of this earth. As soon as

God's plan has been carried out completely, He will call an end to history.

We might think of history as the scaffolding God uses to build His temple. As soon as the temple is complete, He will no longer need the scaffolding, just as He will no longer need the laborers who helped with the building, whether wittingly or unwittingly. That's how important the church is. It was for the church's sake that the great drama on Golgotha took place. And it's because of the church that soldiers by the millions become embroiled in colossal wars.

Everything revolves around the church and furthers the building of the church, even though the church is not mentioned in the first twenty verses of Daniel 11 and is rarely mentioned today in newspapers or reports from the battlefield. How glorious it is to belong to the church, the building that will rise to eternity, the building that will still be standing when there is no trace left of the kingdoms of this earth.

On the other hand, this silence about the Kingdom of God implies an indirect reproach. The time Daniel describes here, the 2nd century before Christ, was a time of spiritual darkness. The voice of the prophets was heard no longer. Israel's expectations of deliverance were fading. The church was becoming worldly, and religion was turning into dead orthodoxy. All of this made it possible for a history of war and military might and injustice to be written without any mention of the church. The people of God were silent, and therefore this page of Scripture is silent about them. What a shame!

> Get you up to a high mountain,
> O Zion, herald of good tidings;
> lift up your voice with strength,
> O Jerusalem, herald of good tidings,
> lift up, fear not;
> say to the cities of Judah,
> "Behold your God!" (Is. 40:9)

32

The Disastrous Abomination

*They will abolish the perpetual sacrifice and install
the disastrous abomination there (11:31 JB).*

IN THE SECOND PART of Daniel 11, we are given an outline of the career of Antiochus Epiphanes, who persecuted the Jews and hated religion. I must emphasize this at the outset, so that we do not waste time focusing our exegetical spotlight on the wrong issue.

When you read this passage, you may be inclined to ask whether Daniel had one of the leaders of our time in mind. To this I can only answer by saying that Daniel has the tyrant Antiochus in mind. Anyone who claims to spot this or that person of our time in this chapter is embarking on a perilous journey, for he is separating the application of the Scriptures from their historical background.

We should not jump to conclusions by identifying some leader of our time with specific Biblical prophecies. Throughout the ages believers have often pointed to figures in their own time as the Antichrist, claiming to see striking resemblances to the descriptions of the Antichrist in the Bible. Both popes and Reformers have been labeled the Antichrist. Serious mistakes have been made because of conclusions reached too hastily.

Furthermore, the person sketched in Daniel 11 is doubtless only a *prefiguration* and *forerunner* of the Antichrist. This means that the Antichrist will not be like him in every last respect. The resemblance is to be sought more in the general impression. Once the Antichrist has actually appeared, the church will say: "We recognize him. His appearance was foretold long ago. We are prepared for his tricks. He won't catch us off guard."

After these preliminary remarks, it's time to turn to the text. The first thing Daniel tells us about this coming dictator is that he is a "wretch" who will not be given "royal honors" (11:21 JB). By this Daniel means that no one will have a high opinion of him at the outset. "He shall come in without warning and obtain the kingdom by flatteries" (vs. 21). Thus, he will come to power through slipperiness and clever devices. "Armies shall be utterly swept away before him" (vs. 22). In other words, the opposition to him will be broken quickly—even "the prince of the covenant," Daniel adds. What he means by this is that not only his opponents but even those who have "covenanted" to enter into an alliance with him will simply be trampled underfoot.

Daniel explains the tyrant's mode of operation as follows: "And from the time that an alliance is made with him he shall act deceitfully; and he shall become strong with a small people" (11:23). Thus, he will come to power despite the fact that he has only a small following. "Without warning he shall come into the richest parts of the province" (vs. 24). Before anyone realizes what he is up to, then, he will succeed in taking control of the richest areas. In the process he will settle numerous scores from the past: "He shall do what neither his fathers nor his fathers' fathers had done." Yet he will be hailed as a generous conqueror with a social conscience, for he will divide up the plunder and booty (vs. 24).

But that's not the end of the story. We are also told that this tyrant will devise plots against these strongholds (11:24). In other words, he will make plans to capture various fortresses. How effective his military measures are becomes apparent when a great war breaks out not long afterward. Daniel prophesies, "And he shall stir up his power and his courage against the king of the South with a great army" (vs. 25). The tyrant comes out of this war a victor.

It's not so much that he is superior in military respects. The king of the south is not defeated on the battlefield alone. Daniel tells us: "Plots shall be devised against him. Even those who eat his rich food shall be his undoing; his army shall be swept away" (11:25-6). The army of the south is defeated because there are traitors within it. It's the age-old story of betrayal on the part of those who have been well treated. Daniel adds that many lives will be lost on the battlefield. Weren't those rich territories and strong fortresses worth the sacrifice of many lives?

The very next verse in this chapter apparently tells us of a time two years later in history. The two powers originally opposed to each other are now on the best of terms. At least, that's how it looks! The two kings are now mentioned together; we learn that they are seated at the same table. "The two kings will be bent on mischief and, sitting at the same table, will lie to each other with advantage to neither" (11:27 NEB).

Thus, the two powerful rulers get together in a friendly way, but what each one has in mind is to outwit the other and take advantage of him. Each wants to destroy the other, but neither admits it. Neither one puts his cards face up on the table. The kings exchanged pleasant words, designed to mask their deepest desires and intentions. Coldly they lie to each other.

Thus, the tyrant uses every possible means to augment his power. Sometimes he uses secrecy and deceit, and at other times open violence. We read: "He will return greatly enriched to his own country" (11:28 JB).

Intoxicated with his own success, he takes measures against the holy covenant (11:28), which means that he is not only interested in conquest but also wants to lash out at the people of God with his sacrilegious hand and interfere with their religion. In fact, it becomes evident that this is the tyrant's chief purpose.

Here, too, this cunning dictator goes to work in a clever way. Later the prophet will return to this point at greater length and show us the true nature of this enemy of God. But first he must tell us something else about his political career: "In due time he will make his way southward again, but this time the outcome will not be as before. The ships of Kittim will oppose him, and he will be worsted" (11:29-30 JB).

Here Daniel speaks of a new round of warfare—but with a different outcome. Just as John makes mention in Revelation of a defeat suffered by the Antichrist at the outset—one of the heads of the beast receives a mortal wound—Daniel also speaks of a setback. Yet this setback is not a definitive defeat. Soon the Antichrist rises again in his full glory, until at the end of time he is finally overthrown through the intervention of Christ Himself and comes to a shameful end.

For the present, he is delayed only temporarily as he marches on to his triumph. As Daniel sees it, he might well have emerged victorious if he had to face only his chosen opponent, but once the "ships of Kittim," a strong naval force from across the sea to the west, enter the fray, he is not equal to the task. Hence, he suffers a defeat.

All he can think of doing after his defeat is continuing something he started earlier: he unleashes all his wrath and fury against the "holy covenant." Daniel informs us: "He will retire and take his furious action against the holy covenant and, as before, will favor those who forsake the holy covenant. Forces of his will come and profane the sanctuary citadel; they will abolish the perpetual sacrifice and install the disastrous abomination there" (11:30-1 JB). Now his real identity is finally uncovered. With all the might at his command, he assaults the "holy covenant." By this Daniel means the ordinances of the covenant—and especially the God of the covenant—that have aroused his fury.

Daniel now prophesies about the various measures that will be taken against the church of the Lord. First of all, this dictator will favor those who have forsaken the holy covenant. He will court the renegades, the traders, those who have turned their backs on the faith. After all, who could he better use to carry out his plan of destroying the church than these traders already within the fortress?

Secondly, he will send his forces to "profane the sanctuary citadel." If he cannot get his way through treason and deceit, he will use brute force instead! O Antichrist, there's no need to rely on force, for the children of God will not resist you. You will not find them carrying concealed weapons. They know they are destined to be led as sheep to the slaughter!

The worst of the Antichrist's tactics is the third: "They will abolish the perpetual sacrifice and install the disastrous abomination there." The "perpetual sacrifice" is taken away: the regular meetings held by believers to offer continual praise and thanks to God will be made impossible. The church buildings will be torn down or turned into dance halls. Perhaps they can be used to house factories. Wouldn't that make a lot of sense? Then we could use them every day! The "disastrous abomination" is substituted for the service of the Lord. In other words, everyone is now required to worship the beast and his sign.

Such is the destroyer of the world and the persecutor of the church whose reflection Daniel already saw in the evening sky in the figure of Antiochus Epiphanes. What son of man—or perhaps a son of the devil—will be revealed to us as this tyrant of Daniel 11 when the world's dying moments finally come? Who will succeed in casting such a long shadow? Will we, or perhaps our children, see him face to face? We simply don't know. But we must be prepared all the same.

Meanwhile, our story is not yet over. Daniel has more details about the Antichrist, as we shall see in the next chapter.

33

Great Was His Fall!

He will meet his end with no one to help him
(11:45 NEB).

WHO IS IT THAT WILL MEET his end alone and helpless? Daniel is still talking about the Antichrist. Whatever dazzling heights he may reach, it will *not* be said of him that his kingdom is forever. This can be said only of Christ. *His* Kingdom is the only one that abides and has a future. All other kingdoms will pass away, including that of the Antichrist: "He will meet his end with no one to help him." The bigger they are, the harder they fall!

Earlier we looked at the great triumphs and power the Antichrist will enjoy. We now bring the story of the Antichrist to a conclusion. We read: "The king will do what he chooses; he will exalt and magnify himself above every god and against the God of gods he will utter monstrous blasphemies" (11:36 NEB).

Here we see once again that he uses his power not so much against men and nations as against God. What would please him most of all would be to drive the King of heaven and earth from His throne. He would conquer heaven itself if he could. Since he cannot, he decides instead—as Paul points out—to establish his own throne in God's temple on earth and pretend that *he* is God. From there he breaks out in "monstrous blasphemies." In his rage he turns to the usual weapons of the powerless!

Strangely enough, God allows this to go on. He still does not appear in His majesty to silence the slanderer who has first silenced everyone else. Daniel even prophesies that this blasphemer will prosper. We'll have to swallow that too! But threatening storm clouds eventually gather. Daniel adds: "...until the time of wrath ends, for what is determined must be done" (11:36 NEB). God bides His time.

The persecutor of the church does not succeed because of his own strength but simply because God's plan—which *must* be fulfilled—leaves room for his success. God's wrath must first be full; the chastisement must reach its full extent. Then the end will come, for God will not chastise His people forever. There will be an end to their suffering. His wrath lasts for a moment, but His grace lasts forever.

God's people, who have forsaken His covenant, may well complain about God withdrawing His favor from them, but in fact they must recognize that He remains the same and abides in His promises. Thus, there is an element of hope in Daniel's words: "All will go well for him *until* the time of wrath ends, for what is determined must be done."

In the meantime, both the church and the world will feel the heavy hand of the Antichrist. Just listen to what Daniel says: "Neither shall he regard the God of his fathers, nor the desire of women" (11:37 KJV). Thus, his reign will be a period of complete godlessness. He will have no sympathy whatsoever for the religion of his fathers but will abolish it by means of the strictest penalties. That's why he is called the *Anti*christ. He cannot be accused of being neither hot nor cold. He has a burning hatred of anything godly, including divine ordinances. Hence Daniel adds that he will disregard the "desire of women."

In Paradise God had said to the woman: "Your desire shall be for your husband," but the Antichrist will seek to overturn this divine decree. The morality of marriage will be one of the ordinances abolished by the Antichrist. What was once called a virtue will then be denounced as a vice, as women are encouraged to desire men other than their husbands. Such developments should not surprise us. Once religion is destroyed, the very foundations of morality start to crumble.

Meanwhile, not every form of worship will be abolished. There will be room for one religion. In fact, that religion will be given a place of honor guaranteed by the sword. Daniel explains: "He shall honor the god of fortresses instead of these; a god whom his father did not know he shall honor with gold and silver, with precious stones and costly gifts" (11:38). This "God of fortresses" is really the god of war!

Not only does the Antichrist kneel down in worship before the altar of this god, he also brings him precious gifts. He taxes people heavily so that he can lavish gold and silver and costly jewels on this god. The world will turn into a gigantic fortress and arsenal—the universal temple of the god of war. Officers and soldiers are the elders and choir boys. The sound of bombs and jet fighters forms the litany of this temple-fortress. We who are about to die salute you, O god of fortresses and war! It's no wonder that the Antichrist ascribes his amazing success to this "foreign god" as he seizes control of even the "strongest fortresses" (11:39).

In this anti-Christian state, human nature shows itself to be stronger than any doctrine. Despite the fact that the Antichrist has fulminated against the corruptness of the old governmental order, he gives the choices possessions to his favourites and the best pieces of land to those who join in his conspiracies. That's what Daniel means when he writes: "Those whom he favors he will load with honor, putting them in the office over the common people and distributing the land at a price" (11:39 NEB).

In *blitzkrieg* style he will go on to conquer the whole world. The kingdom of the Antichrist will become a world empire. He comes, he sees, he conquers. People after people, nation after nation bow before his scepter.

At first there may be a lot of resentment and disgusted hatred of the Antichrist, but this will gradually diminish. Therefore, John writes in Revelation: "The whole world went after the beast in wondering admiration" (Rev. 13:3).

Daniel describes this success for us. Although the traditional enemies mobilize once more and throw all their armies and naval forces into the fight against him, "with chariots and cavalry and mighty ships," he will "overrun land after land, sweeping over them like a flood" (11:40 NEB). This concise description leads us to think that these events will take place in a surprisingly short time.

We also get the impression that the forces of the Antichrist will enjoy an overwhelming numerical superiority as they "overrun" countries and "sweep over" them. People hardly know where the columns of troops stretching further and further than the eye can see have come from so quickly. The soldiers of the Antichrist sweep through country after country like a swarm of locusts. They go on and on and on.

"He shall come into the glorious land," Daniel adds parenthetically (11:41). He then continues: "He shall stretch out his hand against the countries, and the land of Egypt shall not escape" (vs. 42). We're not sorry to hear about Egypt's fate! "The Libyans and the Ethiopians shall follow his train" (vs. 43). We don't mind hearing that they'll get their turn too. But that even the "glorious land," the *holy* land, will fall—that must have bothered Daniel a great deal. The Holy Land was to be trampled underfoot by this conqueror!

As I indicated, Daniel throws in this bit of information in a seemingly parenthetical way. Yet the holy land is in fact his central concern. All those other countries with their hidden stores of gold and silver (11:43) may be seized and may serve as the booty of war, but that the land and people of the Lord, as the Church of Christ, should have to suffer—that's the keystone of this dictator's anti-Christian edifice. It's not without reason that he is called the *Anti*christ!

The Antichrist's identity is also revealed through an interesting note in verse 41: "But these shall be delivered out of his hand: Edom and Moab and the main part of the Ammonites." After the long list of nations that fall to the power of the Antichrist, these are the only ones to escape his domination. Why does he spare these nations, of all the nations?

Anyone familiar with the scriptures knows the answer. Edom, Moab, and Ammon were the traditional enemies of the people of God. The children of God and all who sympathize with them are the ones who will feel the brutal power of the Antichrist. But the sworn enemies of the people of God will still be allowed a relative independence. The true colours of the Antichrist are to be seen in his choice of favourites.

The bigger they are, the harder they fall. When the Antichrist is overthrown, then, he will be in for a rough landing. And Daniel shows us that this is indeed the case: "Rumors from the east and the north will alarm him, and he will depart in a great rage to destroy and exterminate many. He will pitch his royal pavilion between the sea [the great sea, the Mediterranean] and the holy hill [Mount Zion], the fairest of all hills; and he will meet his end with no one to help him" (11:44-5 NEB).

What finally leads to his fall is a rumor—public enemy number one. We are not told anything about the rumor. Perhaps it is a rumor to the effect that revolution has broken out back home. The dictator then sets out to destroy and exterminate many—activities he seems to enjoy greatly. But this time the use of force proves futile. While his royal pavilion, a virtual palace, is pitched between Jerusalem and the Mediterranean Sea and serves as his headquarters, the end comes unexpectedly. His end is just as sudden as his rise.

Daniel does not tell us just how this will come about. He only assures us that there will definitely be an end to the Antichrist's reign, and that there will be no one to help him when he is overthrown. How he will meet his end we learn elsewhere in the scriptures. Christ Himself will appear before the terrified eyes of the Antichrist and slay him with "the breath of His mouth." With one sudden stroke, the Antichrist will be finished, and Jesus will replace him.

If someone should ask how it is possible for the Antichrist, whose life and career were such a success, to reach the end of the line so unexpectedly, there is a simple answer. The Antichrist turns against the "holy covenant," the covenant between God and His people. That covenant cannot be broken. Nations can be conquered and the covenants or treaties between them shattered, but anyone who tries to destroy the "holy covenant" will ultimately destroy himself, however powerful he may be. Not even the devil could get away with it. The mountains may move, and the hills may tremble, but God's covenant will remain unshaken.

The holy covenant gives security to the church, the "glorious land." The Antichrist may take his headquarters temporarily in the holy land, but he will have to surrender his claim to it before long.

The final victory belongs to the church—not because it is so strong but because it has such a strong and faithful covenant partner. It is because of this covenant that the heavens will eventually open. Then truth, justice, peace, and faithfulness will rule on the earth.

34

Deliverance

At that time shall arise Michael, the great prince who has charge of your people. And there shall be a time of trouble, such as never has been since there was a nation till that time; but at that time your people shall be delivered, everyone whose name shall be found written in the book. And many of those who sleep in the dust of the earth shall awake, some to everlasting life, and some to shame and everlasting contempt. And those who are wise shall shine like the brightness of the firmament; and those who turn many to righteousness, like the stars forever and ever. But you, Daniel, shut up the words, and seal the book, until the time of the end. Many shall run to and fro, and knowledge shall increase (12:1-4).

THERE ARE ALL SORTS OF HORRIBLE, fearful prophecies in the book of Daniel. We read about wars and nations in turmoil. All of this leads to the rule of the Antichrist, under which the *church* will suffer particularly. Of course, the story *cannot* end there. The enemy of God and His church cannot and may not have the last word!

The book of Daniel is gospel, good news, a proclamation of the triumph of Christ! Consequently, the final chapter of the book includes a song of deliverance—in words that we would almost expect to read in the New Testament instead: "At that time your people shall be delivered, everyone whose name shall be found written in the book. And many of those who sleep in the dust of the earth shall awake"!

To make the light of deliverance shine even brighter, Daniel once more shows us the dark background. "There shall be a time of trouble such as never has been since there was a nation till that time." This somber prophecy points beyond Antiochus Epiphanes to the great tribulation under the Antichrist. The Savior Himself also thought in these terms. In words reminiscent of Daniel, He declared: "It will be a time of great distress; there has never been such a time from the beginning of the world until now, and will never be again. If that time of troubles were not cut short, no living thing could survive" (Matt. 24:21-2 NEB).

Thus, the last days will be very difficult for the people of the Lord. We will no longer be able to go to church and draw strength from communion with God and each other, for public worship services will be banned. Those who confess the name of Christ will be boycotted, for only those who bear the mark of the beast will be able to buy and sell. Day after day, God's children will be subjected to the most horrible blasphemy. The blood of the martyrs will flow as never before.

But however dark God's ways may be, His church will not go under. He will not permit His holy ones to be destroyed. "At that time your people shall be delivered."

We don't need to wonder where deliverance will come from. The people of God will be saved not through the heroism of their own faith or through their courageous perseverance but only through Christ. All the same, Christ does make use of certain means to preserve His own and enable them to survive to the end. The *usual* means are the Word and the sacraments. We should attach *unusual* significance to them, for the time will come when they are taken away. In the time of which Daniel speaks here, there will be no more preaching of the Word and administration of the sacraments.

In this extraordinary period, the Lord will employ extraordinary means to keep His church from going under. If escape to the right and left and every other direction is cut off, there's only one way left: we must look for help from above. God's angels will arrive from above when they come to rescue us. "At that time shall rise Michael, the great prince who has charge of your people." That Michael and the angels at his command "have charge of your people" means that it is their special task to protect the people of the Lord. At the right moment, the legions from heaven will take up their positions alongside the weary warriors on earth.

Daniel does not tell us exactly how this help will be sent. But just as evil spirits influence the children of this world in an invisible way, the power of God's angels will animate the holy ones in those last days and give them superhuman spiritual power. Just as an angel strengthened Jesus in Gethsemane, His followers will be given the strength to drink the cup of suffering when they are being dragged down the road to the cross.

There are still angels in the air—and not just wicked spiritual powers, bombers and jet fighters. Could anyone really believe that God's invincible army would sleep when all the wicked powers in the air are mobilized against Christ's lambs? Those shining figures are there, whether we see them or not. Who can say how much we already owe them and how many dangers we have escaped because of their intervention?

Actually, we ought to be the most thankful not to the angels but to Christ. *He* refused their help when they were standing ready behind heaven's curtain. He wanted them to be sent out instead to help those who were to inherit salvation. *He* struggled with demons so that *we*, for His sake, could be surrounded by angels.

Those angels keep watch over us. They drive evil spirits away and direct our eyes toward heaven. When the last battle has been fought, they will bring God's children to Abraham's bosom.

Those who will be saved when the great deliverance comes are characterized by Daniel as the ones "whose names shall be found written in the book." The book he refers to, of course, is the Lamb's book of life. Jesus, too, spoke of names recorded in heaven. In this book are the names of all those whom God recognizes as His own—but not all those whom we expect to find in heaven. *Man* can see externals only, but *the Lord* sees into our hearts.

Those who enjoy this inestimable privilege are sinners, for it is the Lamb's book. Their names appear in it not because of anything they have done but because of the Lamb, whose blood has washed away all their sins. No one whose name is recorded in heaven has any reason to act proud. The Savior asks us to rejoice and be amazed that even *our* names appear in the book. Praise God for the wonder of His grace!

Here on earth, we have a copy of the heavenly book of life—the Bible. We cannot read God's own book of life, but we can certainly read the Bible. If we will only think of ourselves whenever we see a reference to "sinners" and "godless people," we will be able to read our own names in it clearly.

The greatness of the deliverance that the church of the Lord will enjoy one day is apparent from what the angel next says to Daniel: "And many of those who sleep in the dust of the earth shall wake, some to everlasting life, and some to shame and everlasting contempt." Through this double contrast, we are given an indication of the glory of the children of God.

The first contrast is that of death. The angel speaks of those who sleep in the dust of the earth. In a monotony barren of any comfort, grave after grave is dug. Hardly have we emerged from one period of mourning then we are plunged into another. But listen! I hear the sound of the last trumpet! Those who sleep in the dust of the earth will awake! And what an awakening that will be! That glorious morning will never be followed by evening. On that day we will exchange our sinner's rags for the beautiful garments of sanctified saints.

The second contrast is the entirely different fate awaiting those who do not believe: they will awaken to shame and everlasting contempt. They, too, will be reunited with their bodies—monstrously misshapen bodies rather than glorified bodies. Theirs will be bodies in which the full horror and ugliness of sin is reflected, bodies they will find revolting.

"And those who are wise shall shine like the brightness of the firmament." God did not intend this promise as an epitaph for preachers and professors. When Daniel speaks of "those who are wise," he means those who remained faithful during the time of tribulation by continuing to testify about the Savior. It may be that they are very simple people; he goes on to speak of "those who turn many to righteousness."

Through their godly way of life, they win their neighbors for Christ! On the day of resurrection, they will not be given special glory, but they will shine like the brightness of the firmament, like the stars. They will finally be seen as what they have already become in principle in this life—guiding stars that serve to show many mariners the way to the distant land across the sea.

"But you, Daniel, shut up the words, and seal the book, until the time of the end." The purpose of this command was not to keep the contents of the book a secret. Daniel was to seal the book so that he would be able to preserve it as a precious document, just as valuables are locked in the safe. He was to do so "until the time of the end." When the time has actually come, when the day of tribulation arrives, many people "will be at their wits' end" (12:4 NEB).

The Word of God is not a book to be read through quickly or to glance at in passing after a meal. We must learn to search the Scriptures thoroughly, looking for redemptive promises. Only in this way, Daniel informs us, will "knowledge increase." By searching the Scriptures, we will be able to increase our knowledge of how God leads His people in history in an amazing way, and we will draw comfort from this knowledge in the dark circumstances of our lives. Even in days of tribulation, the church of the Lord will be able to sing about the wonders of God's grace.

35

How Long?

How long shall it be till the end of these wonders?
(12:6).

THERE MUST HAVE BEEN great joy in Daniel's heart as he listened to the message of his people's deliverance. Yet, imagine his pain as he contemplated the prospect of the severe tribulation that would come before the deliverance. This led him to ask how long that horrible, anti-Christian period would last: "How long shall it be till the end of these wonders?" He was correct in speaking here of "wonders," for it seemed surprising an inexplicable that the Lord would subject His people to virtual destruction.

The prophet got a prompt answer to his question: he was told that "it would be for a time, two times, and a half a time; and that when the shattering of the power of the holy people comes to an end and all these things would be accomplished" (12:7). Whether this answer fully satisfied Daniel we do not know. In any event, it was an answer. In actual fact, it gave him more than he had asked for, for he was told not only about the duration of the tribulation but also what it would be like.

The period in which the Antichrist persecutes the church will be the time when the great antagonist carries out his plan of breaking the power of the people of God. In other words, he will seek to crush the power of the holy people. By the "holy people," of course, I mean the holy, Christian church. It is now said of this church that it is a *power* in the world—a *spiritual* power. Wherever there is faith, there is power. True faith has a strengthening and renewing effect on all spheres of society.

The Antichrist cannot tolerate this power. Not only does it stand in the way of his own aspirations, it dares to condemn them. Therefore, he does not rest until he has broken the power of the church, until he has wiped out its influence.

His attack on the church will have a devastating effect. The leaders of the church will be removed from their positions or cast into prison. All instruction, whether oral or written, will be abolished. In no way will the church be allowed to influence the life of society. Through these means, the power of the holy people will indeed be "shattered."

Yet, God's people will not be entirely powerless, for they will still be able to fold their hands in prayer. That will remain their ultimate power. This, then, is what Daniel found out about the nature of the anti-Christian period.

As far as its duration is concerned, he was told that the end of the tribulation would come after "a time, two times, and half a time." Now, it cannot be denied that this is a rather vague answer to Daniel's question. In fact, one might wonder whether it is an answer at all. Apparently, Daniel himself also found the answer perplexing, for he reformulated the question: "I heard, but I did not understand. Then I said, 'O my lord, what shall be the issue of these things?'" (12:8).

In a certain sense, the answer must be seen as God's *refusal* to answer. Even for the prophets, who are privileged to receive revelations about the future, there are limits. Jesus declared that no one knows the hour of His return. Therefore, we can hardly expect an angel to tell it to Daniel. The answer was withheld from Daniel because he did not need to know it.

Yet, what he did need to know was in fact revealed to him: the angel's words about a time, two times and half a time have a deeper meaning. When the Angel speaks of a certain time, he is referring to the period when the Antichrist establishes his dominion. Once the Antichrist is firmly in the saddle, the second period of his rule begins. This is what the angel means when he speaks of two times or a double time. In this period, the affliction is doubled, and the burden borne by the believers grows much heavier. The promises of peace and prosperity made to the church remain unfulfilled during this time of tribulation. In fact, the suffering of the church increases steadily.

But this period is still not the end. A third period will dawn. In this last period, the power of the church on earth will be broken completely. The church will then be without any influence. But just when the church's situation seems to be totally hopeless, deliverance will be at hand. Just when the Antichrist reaches the culmination of his power, he will suddenly be toppled. In the midst of his wrathful raging, he will be slain by the breadth of Christ's mouth. This is the redemptive symbolism behind the phrase "half a time." The tyrant is shut down in full flight, so to speak.

This answer will have to satisfy Daniel. A more exact knowledge of all the times and numbers will make little difference. The one thing that really matters is to know that Christ will eventually deliver His chosen ones in their hour of peril. The people of God may lose all their power on earth, but the Lord's strong right hand is capable of intervention at any moment.

It was not by chance that the angel who told Daniel all these things stood above the river or water. In God's Word, rivers or waters are frequently used to symbolize the might of the nations. These rivers may believe they can flow right over God's people, but the Lord's throne is established forever above all the rivers and seas. The Lord of hosts is His name!

The angel sealed the promise by swearing an oath by the One who lives forever. This settles the matter, for the cause of the church has become God's cause. Hence the persecution of the church is a direct attack on God. Such an affront cannot be permitted. The Lord sometimes lets His children sink, but He does not let them drown, as Luther pointed out.

As I indicated earlier, the prophet raised his question again, even though the angel had given an extensive answer. Thus prophets, too, are sometimes slow to understand. "I heard, but I did not understand. Then I said, 'O my lord, what shall be the issue of these things?'"

The angel could have responded by saying, "Be quiet, Daniel, for what I have already told you is enough." But he didn't do that. Patiently he went into the matter once more. He said: "Go your way, Daniel, for the words are kept secret and sealed till the time of the end" (12:9 NEB).

We should be thankful for this considerate answer, for it adds to the assurance already given. Earlier Daniel was told that it would be possible to survive the period of tribulation, and now he is told *how* it is possible. Don't worry about it, Daniel. Just go your own way, for "the words are kept secret and sealed till the time of the end."

This is a most encouraging assurance. They may be able to take away our bread, our churches, and even our lives, but they will never cancel God's Word and promises. These promises are sealed and will be carefully preserved.

This is puzzling language for anyone who regards God's Word as secondary rather than primary. He will think to himself, "That Word is no substitute for food and drink. Where will I get my daily bread?" Yet it is a proclamation of great joy for all who have experienced the power and comfort of the living Word. They thank God that neither life nor death can separate us from that Word. We can always count on the protection afforded by God's hand and the favor of His countenance. That should be enough for any child of God.

At the conclusion of his response to Daniel's question, the angel declared that the anti-Christian period would last 1290 days. He added: "Blessed is he who stands firm and attains a thousand three hundred and thirty-five days" (12:12 JB).

These are rather mysterious words. Earlier we noted that the dawning of the day of the Lord cannot be calculated in advance. Thus, the angel did not intend to give us a date that can be marked on our calendar. Here, too, the Bible is speaking in figurative language.

When we start to puzzle over what these words mean, we notice first of all that the length of the final struggle is reckoned in *days*. The angel gives us numbers, indicating that we will be counting the days when the end draws near. Thus, we are clearly given to understand that the oppression of the church will not be a matter of centuries or generations but only of days. The suffering believers will simply have to take courage and wait patiently on the Lord. There will certainly be some very difficult days, but they will only be *days*. One by one we can mark them off on the calendar.

Take courage! Blessed is he who perseveres, who survives all of this, who stands firm for the entire 1335 days and does not despair. The Lord Jesus strips those prophetic words of their figurative meaning by a clear and concise revelation: "The man who stands firm to the end will be saved" (Matt. 24:13 JB).

The book of Daniel ends with these remarkable words: "But go your way to the end and rest, and you shall rise to your destiny at the end of the age" (12:13 NEB). This concluding sentence contains both a command and a promise. Daniel is told to go his way, to continue fighting the good fight, to persevere to the end. The promise is that when the end comes, he will realize his destiny and receive his share of the inheritance of the saints.

This personal statement is a thrilling conclusion especially for such a book as Daniel. This book reveals something of God's plan for the world and the church. We are shown both horrible and glorious things about the last days. In chilling language, the great conflict between Christ and the Antichrist is described.

At the very end we come to this rather intimate statement addressed to Daniel personally. The angel is telling Daniel:

"Don't get bogged down in all sorts of speculative questions. Don't make the mistake of supposing that the sole purpose of these revelations is too deep for your insight into prophetic matters. Shedding light on various specific points is useful and necessary, but the most important thing is how the revelation affects you personally, Daniel. You must ask yourself what the Lord means to say to you in particular."

The angel's instructions to Daniel also apply to us. Have we understood this book that way? I have written these pages to further just such an understanding of these prophecies. Whatever trials and struggles we may face in the future, the study of the book of Daniel should leave us convinced that the Word of God will abide forever. Jesus Christ is the same yesterday, today, and forever. Amen.

www.ingramcontent.com/pod-product-compliance
Lightning Source LLC
Chambersburg PA
CBHW031407290426
44110CB00011B/290